RD Riccoboni, From Old Town to New Town, The San Diego Paintings

Beacon Artworks Gallery

RD Riccoboni®
From Old Town to New Town
The San Diego Paintings

Published by Beacon Artworks Corporation 2009
1010 University Avenue, Suite 474
San Diego, California 92103 USA

Paperback ISBN 978-0-578-03590-1

Printed and bound in The United States of America

In ths book take a tour through historic San Diego with one of America's favorite artists, RD Riccoboni, as you enjoy paintings of many of the city's historic settings such as Old Town, Balboa Park, Downtown's Gaslamp, Coronado Island, La Jolla, along with other California landscapes and seascapes that dance with color and life seen from different perspectives and contrasts.

Old Town – New Town San Diego, The Paintings of RD Riccoboni are selections from the Beacon Artworks Collection. Many of these paintings are on exhibit at Beacon Artworks Gallery located in Fiesta de Reyes at Old Town San Diego State Historic Park.

RD Riccoboni tells the story of California, notably San Diego, from Old Town to today. Old Town - New Town is the name of the on-going exhibition and this book contains selections from the show created by Mr. Riccoboni between 2005 to 2009.

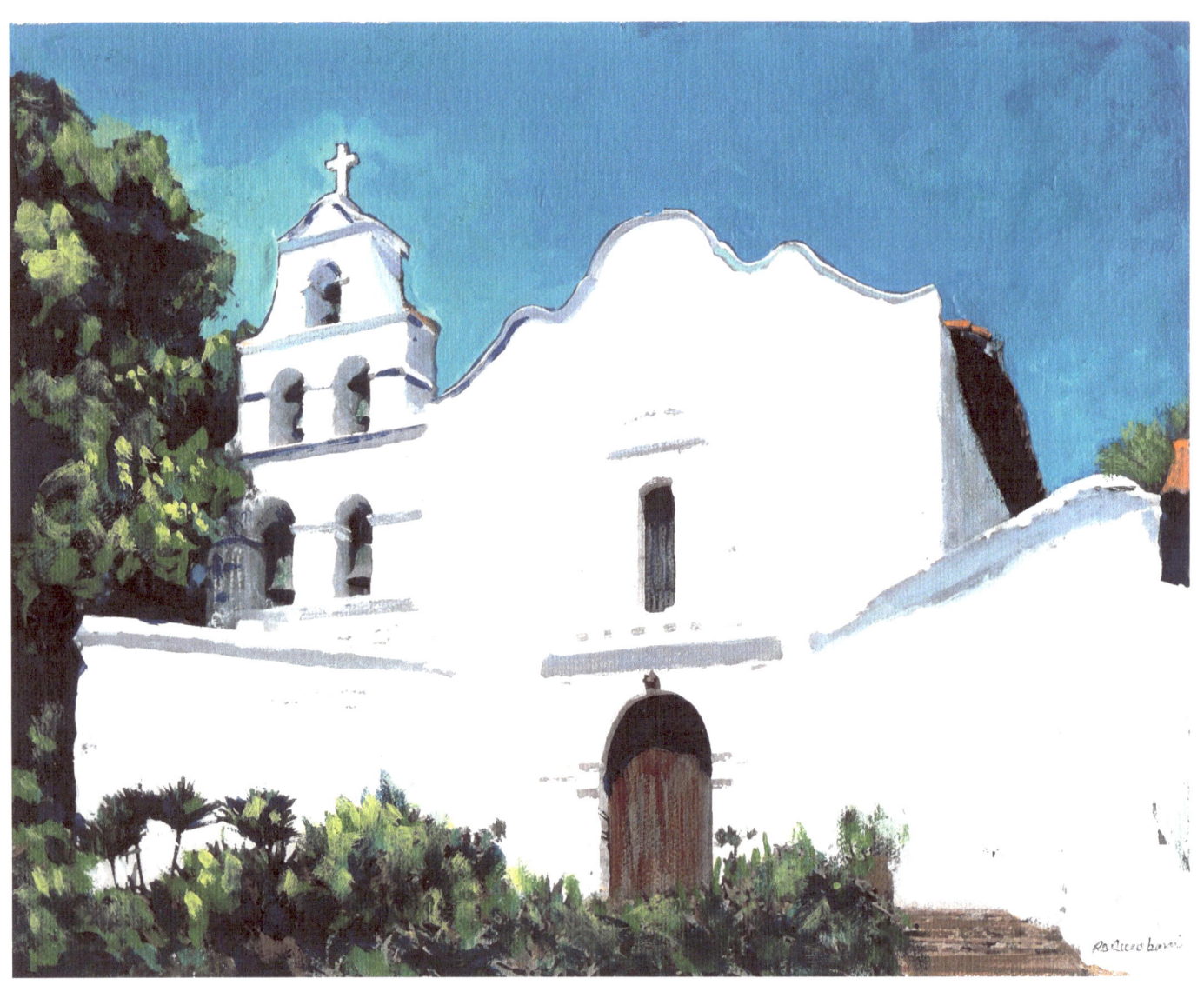

Above: **San Diego Mission de Alcala**.

Right: **Mission Interior**
the San Diego Mission de Alcala

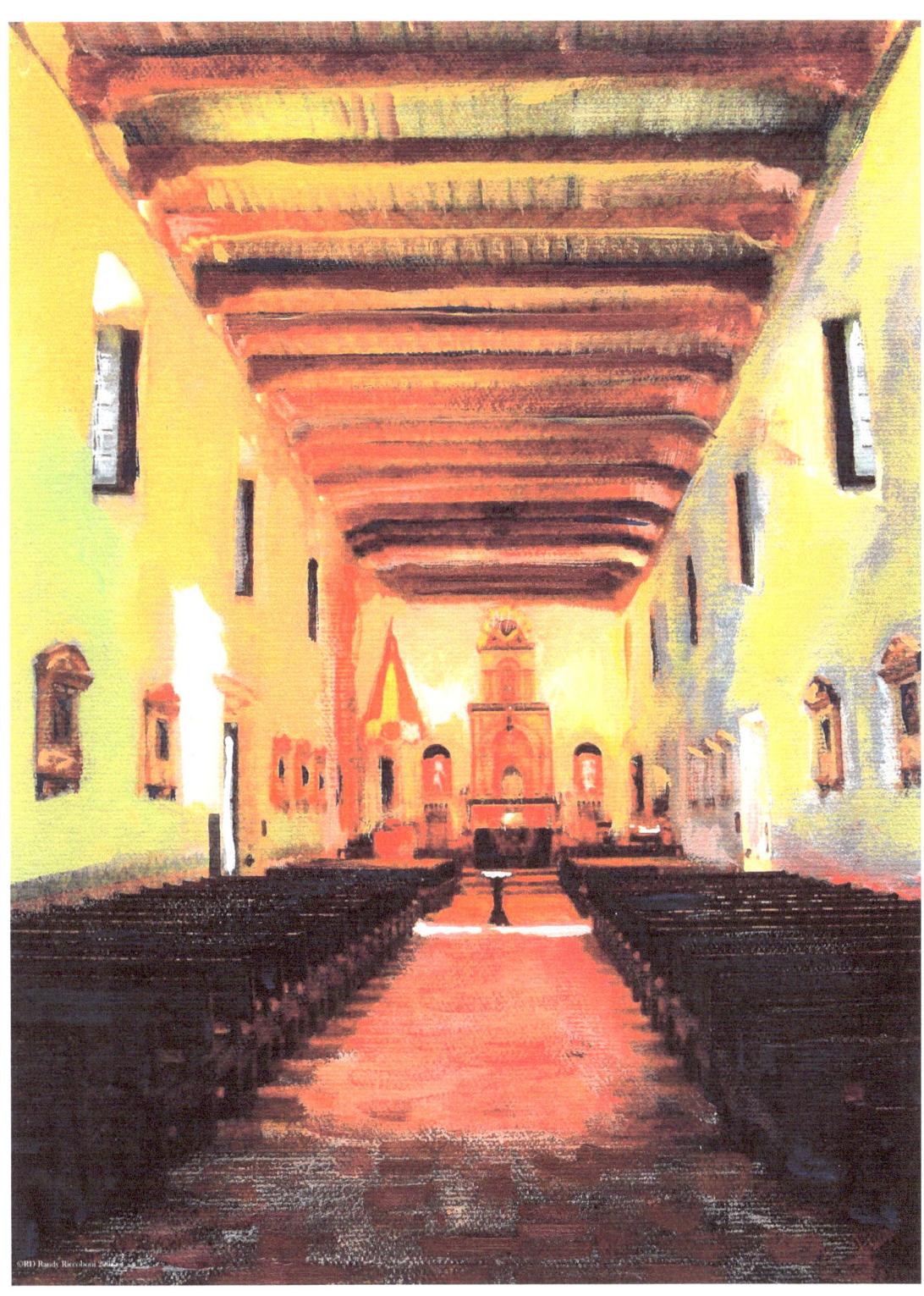

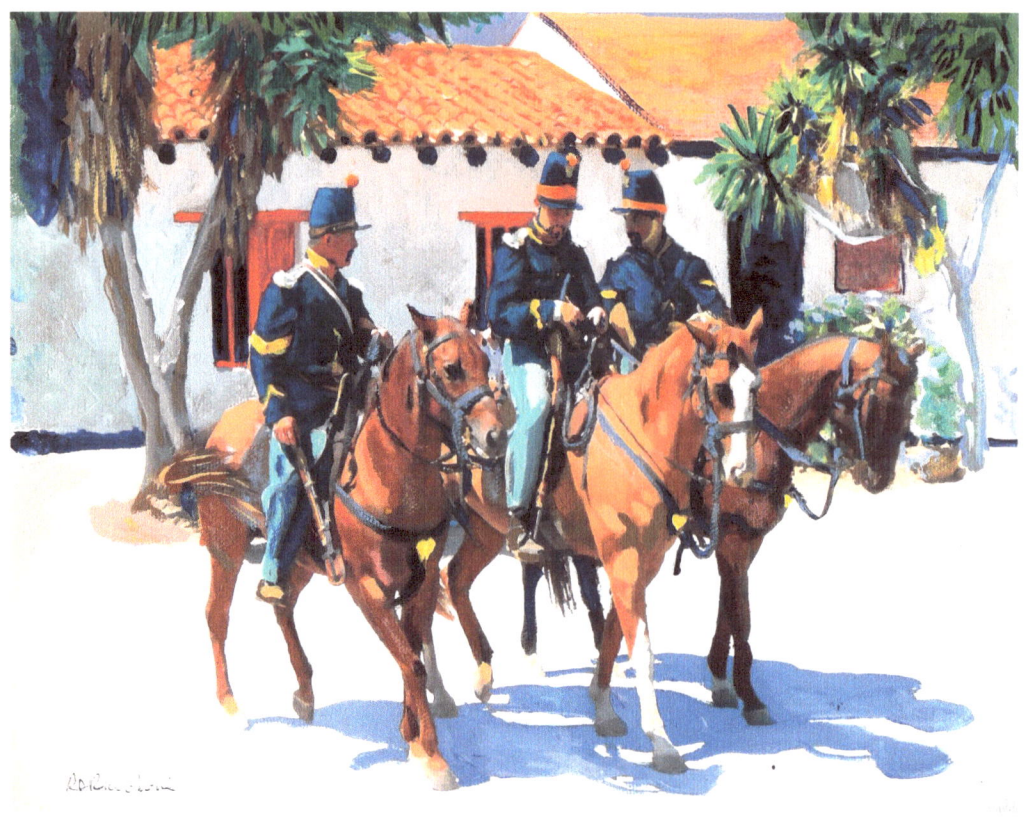

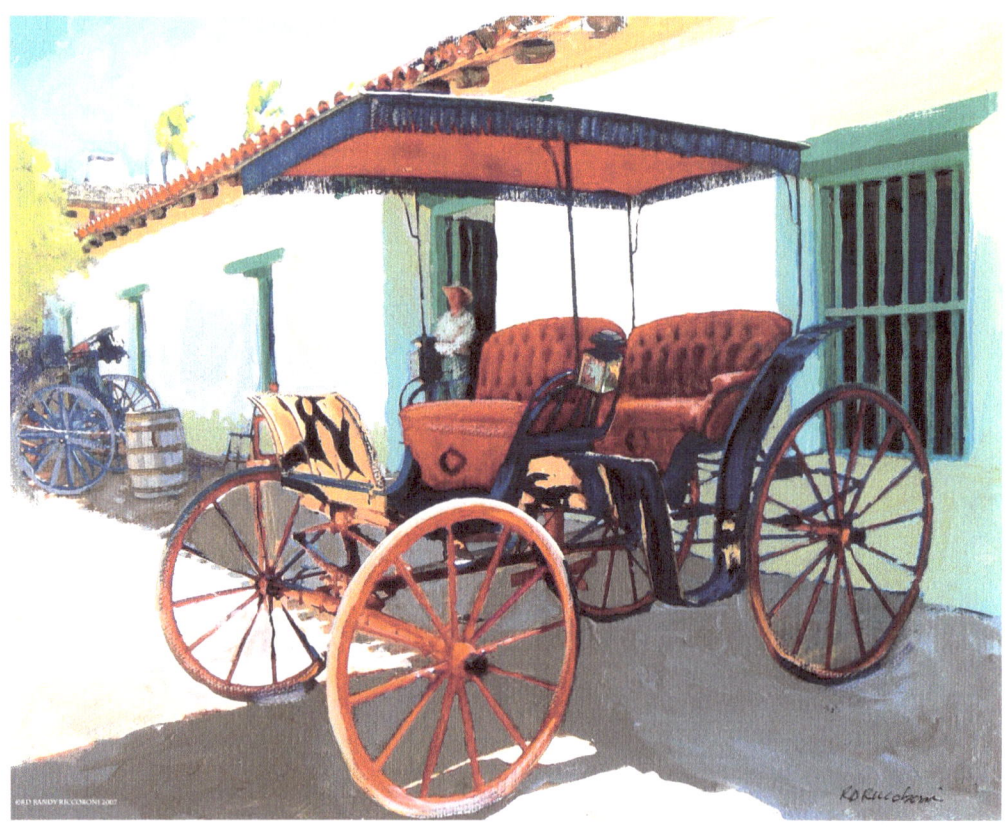

Above: ***U.S. Army Dragoons on San Diego Avenue in Old Town***

Below: ***Surrey with the Fringe on Top*** - Old Town San Diego

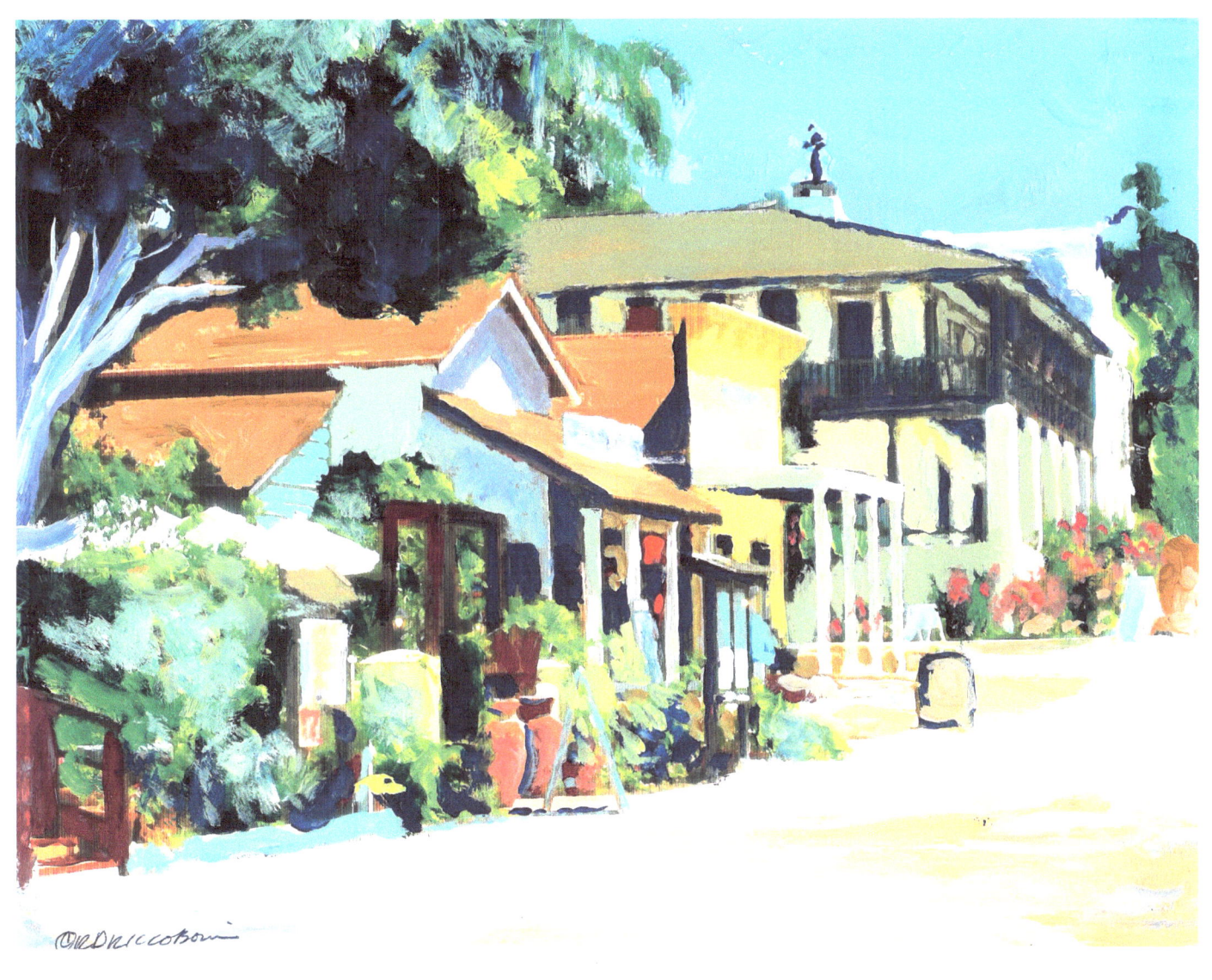

Calhoun Street
Old Town San Diego California

The Alvarado House, Johnson house and
Cosmopolitan Hotel.

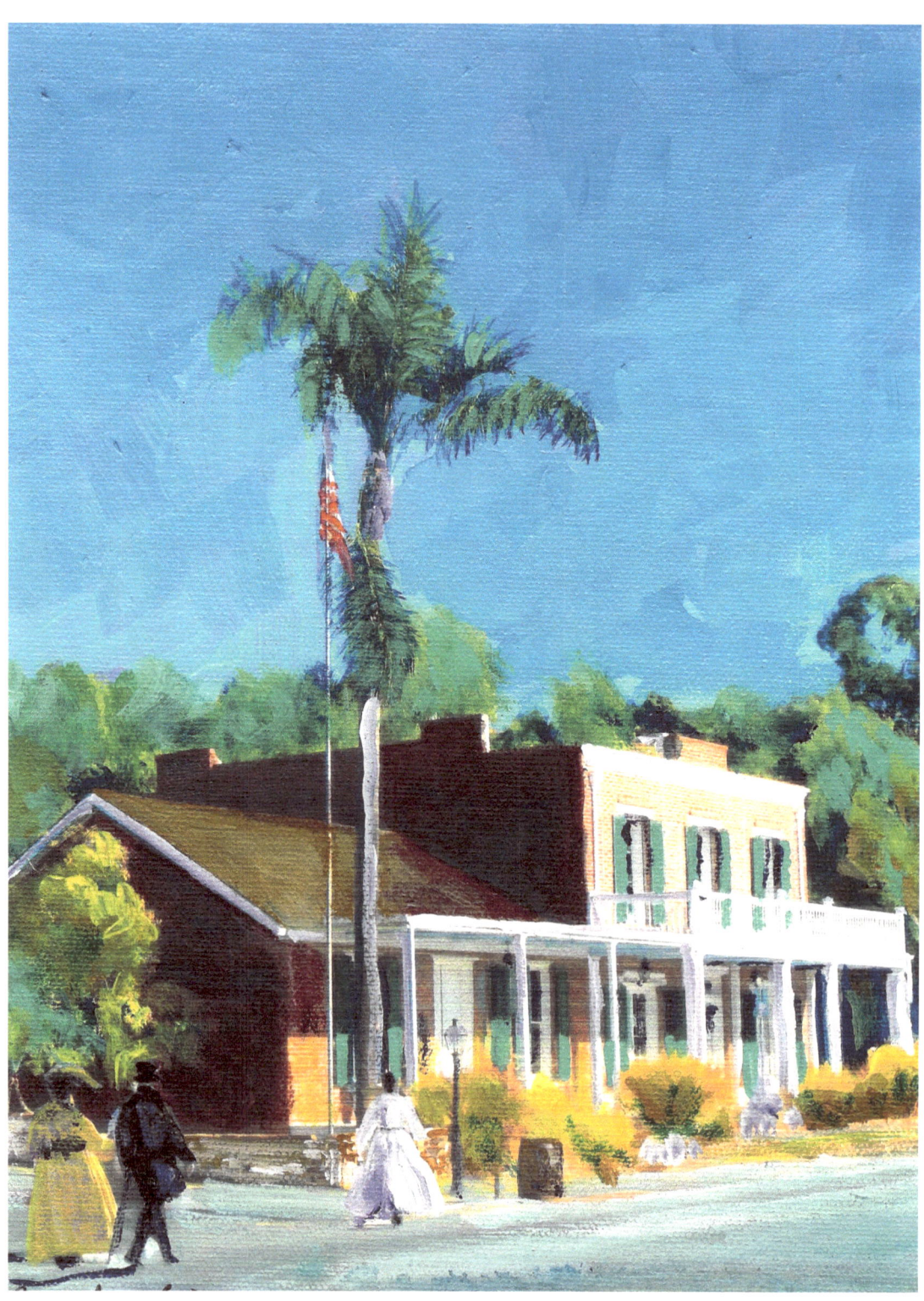

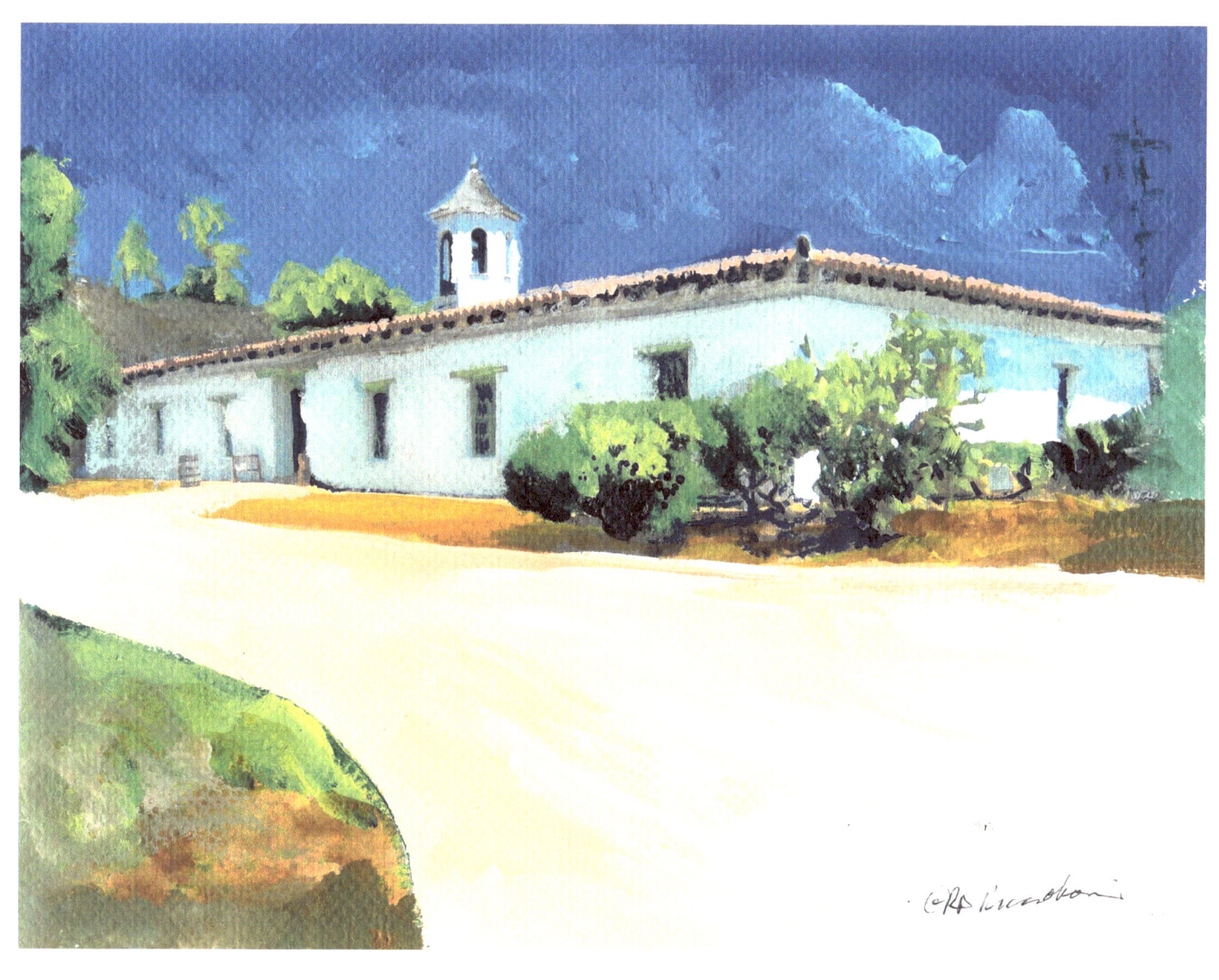

Page Left, **The Whaley House**,
San Diego Avenue, Old Town San Diego

Above: **La Casa de Estidillo**
Old Town San Diego

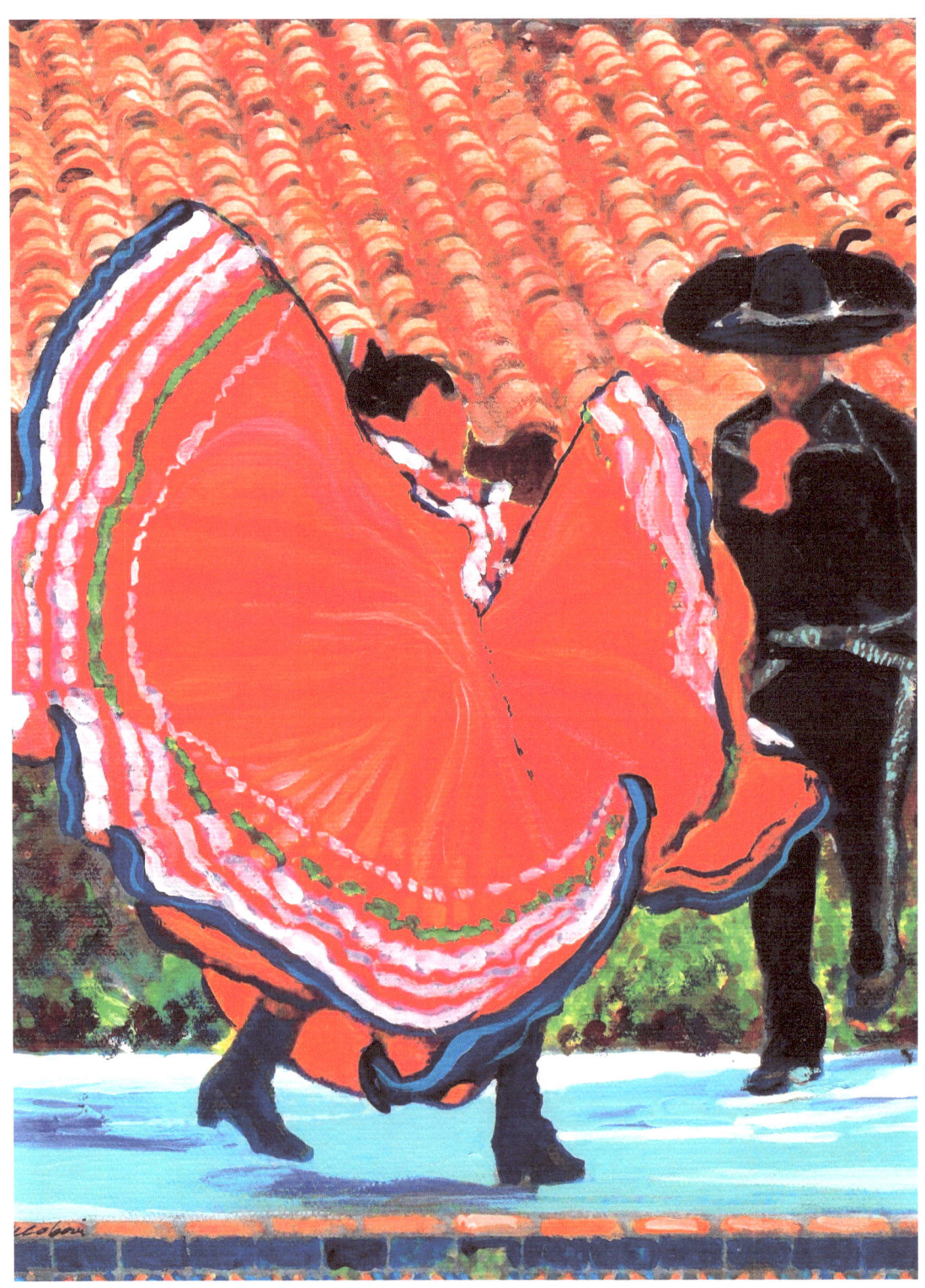

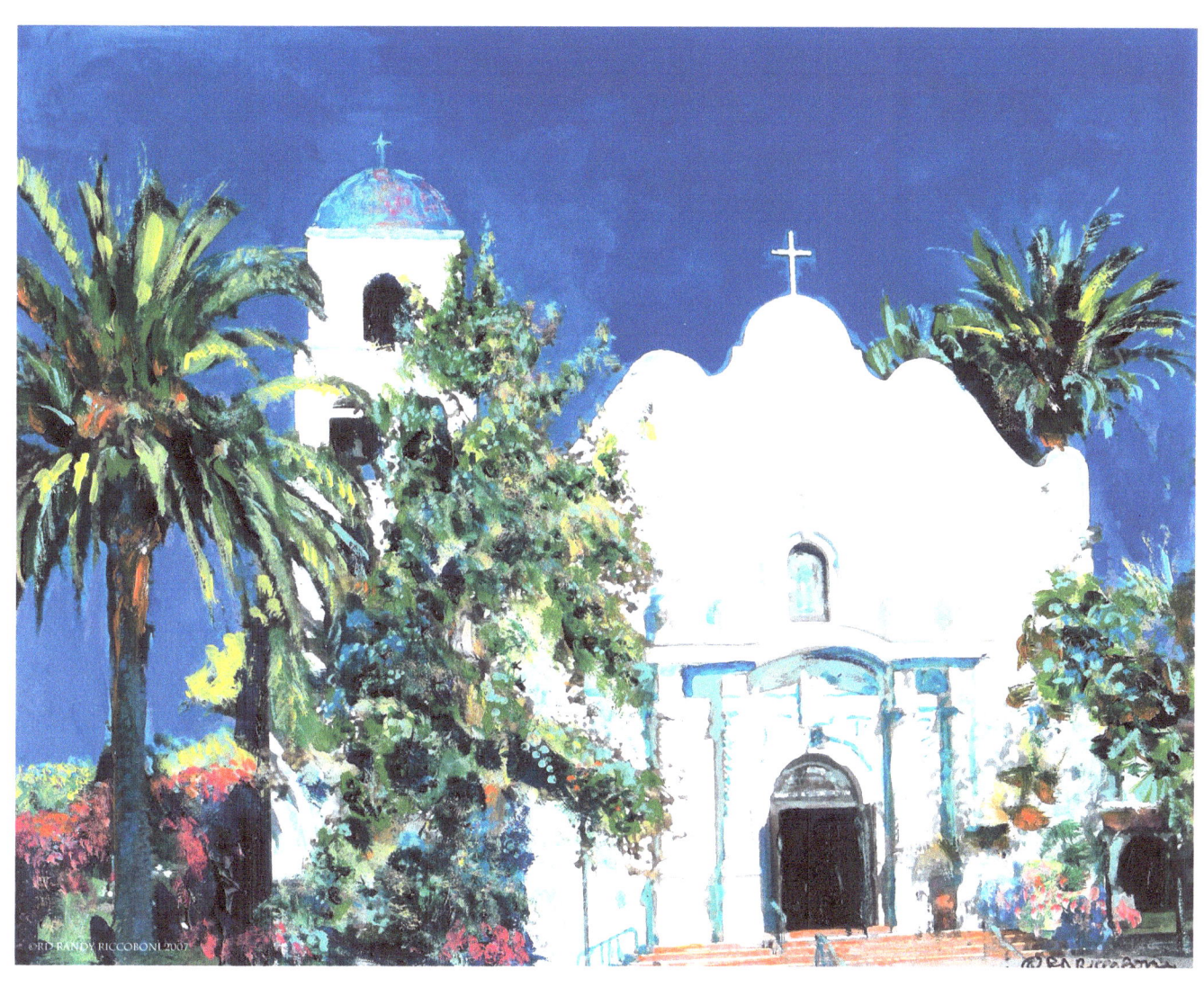

Left. ***Dancer's in Old Town***,

Above, ***Immaculate Church on San Diego Avenue***
Old Town San Diego.

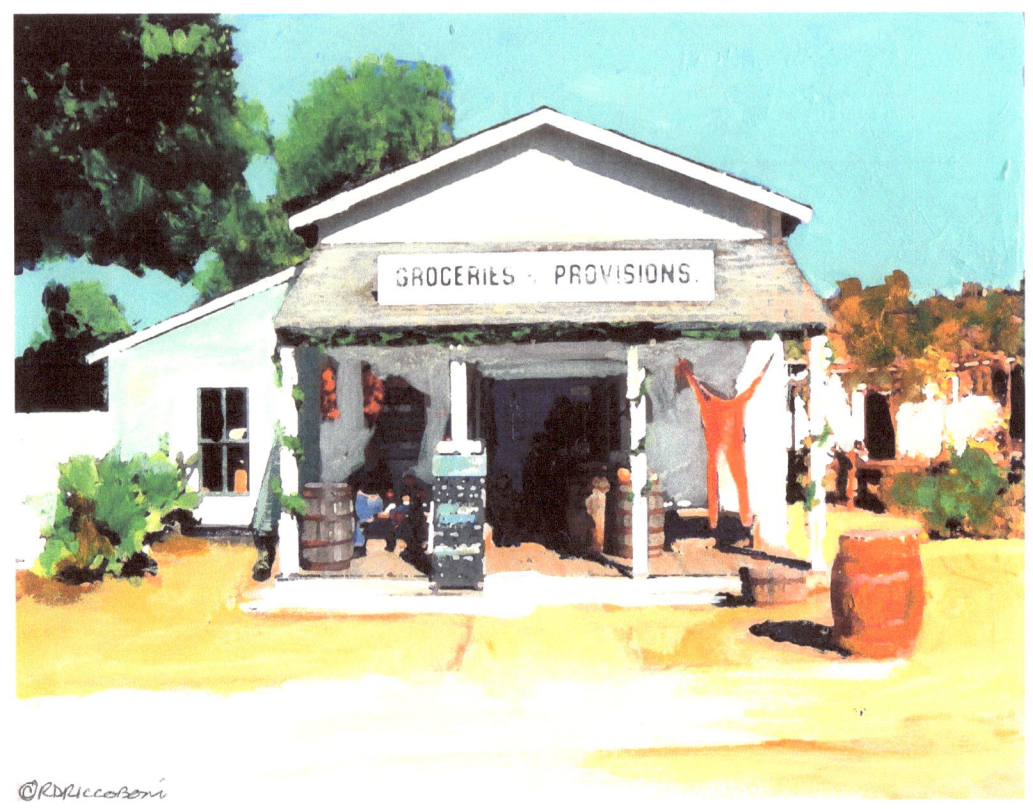

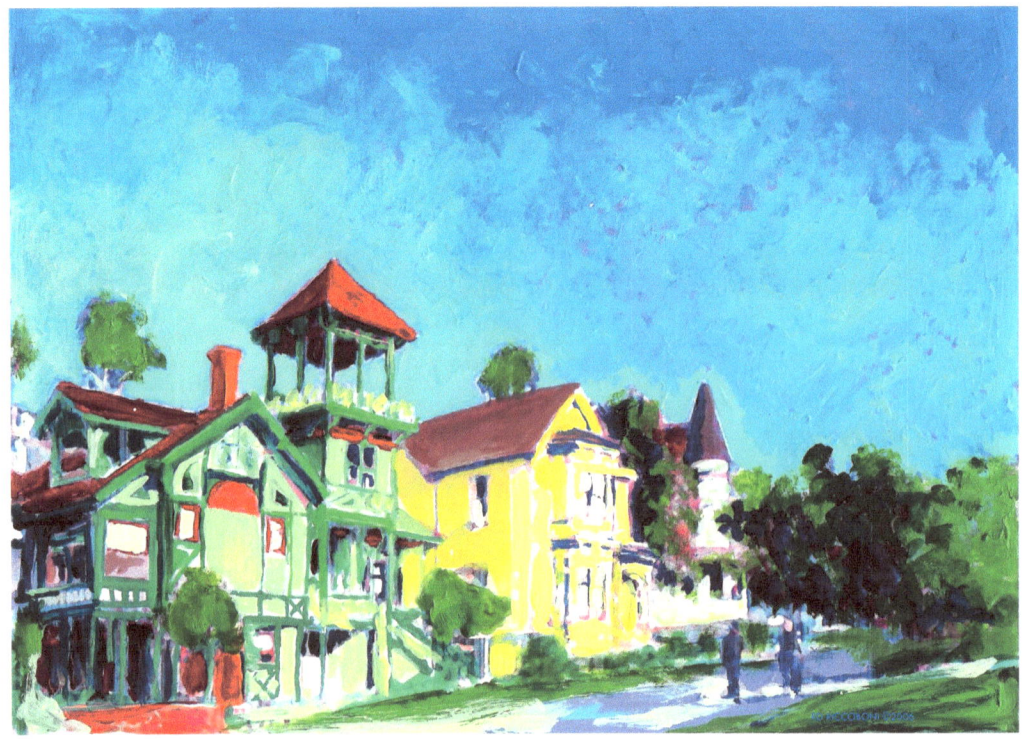

Above: *The Alvarado House*

Below: *Heritage Park Row* in Old Town San Diego. The Sherman Gilbert House, The Bushyhead House and the Christian House.

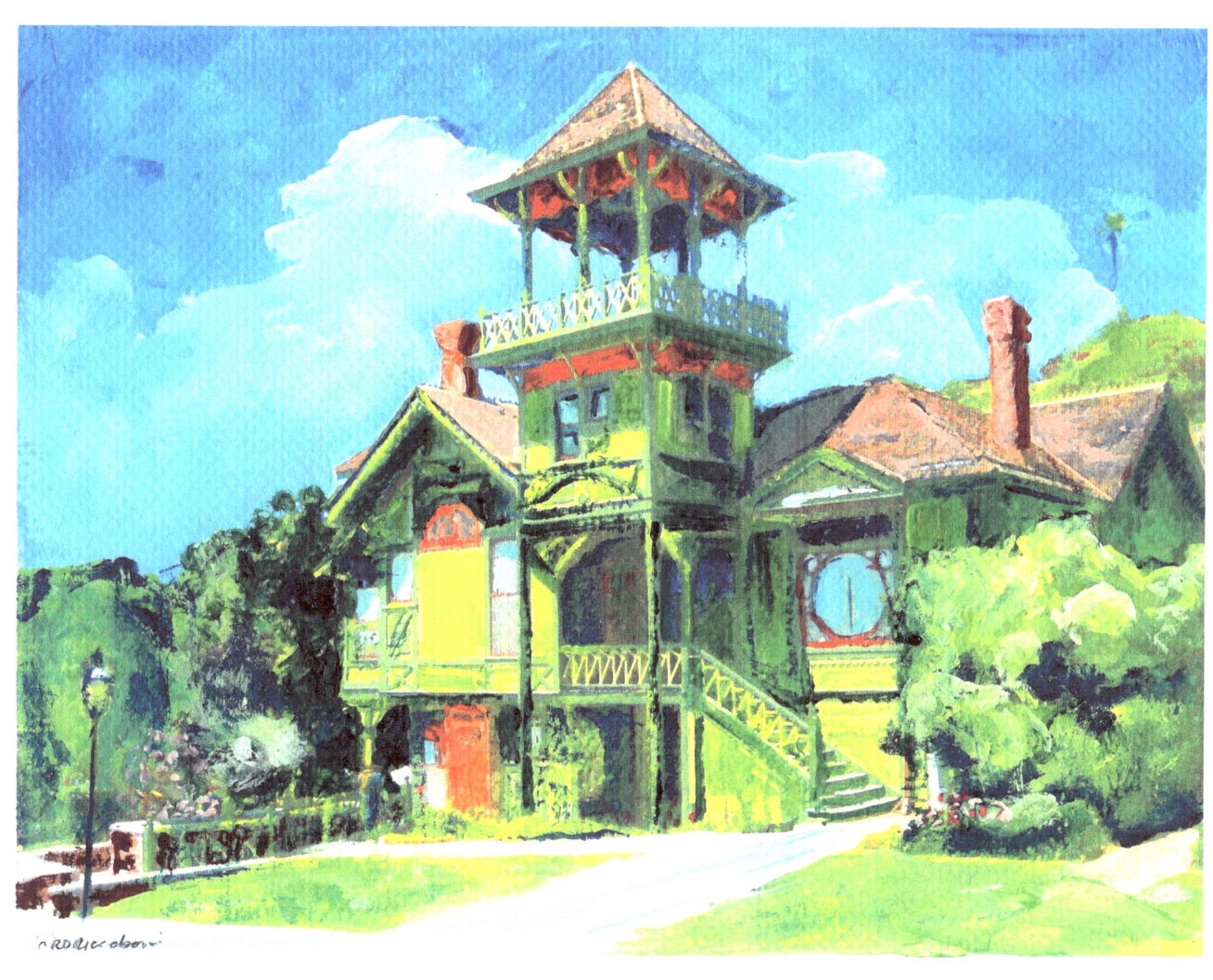

The Sherman Gilbert House
Heritage Park in Old Town San Diego,
California

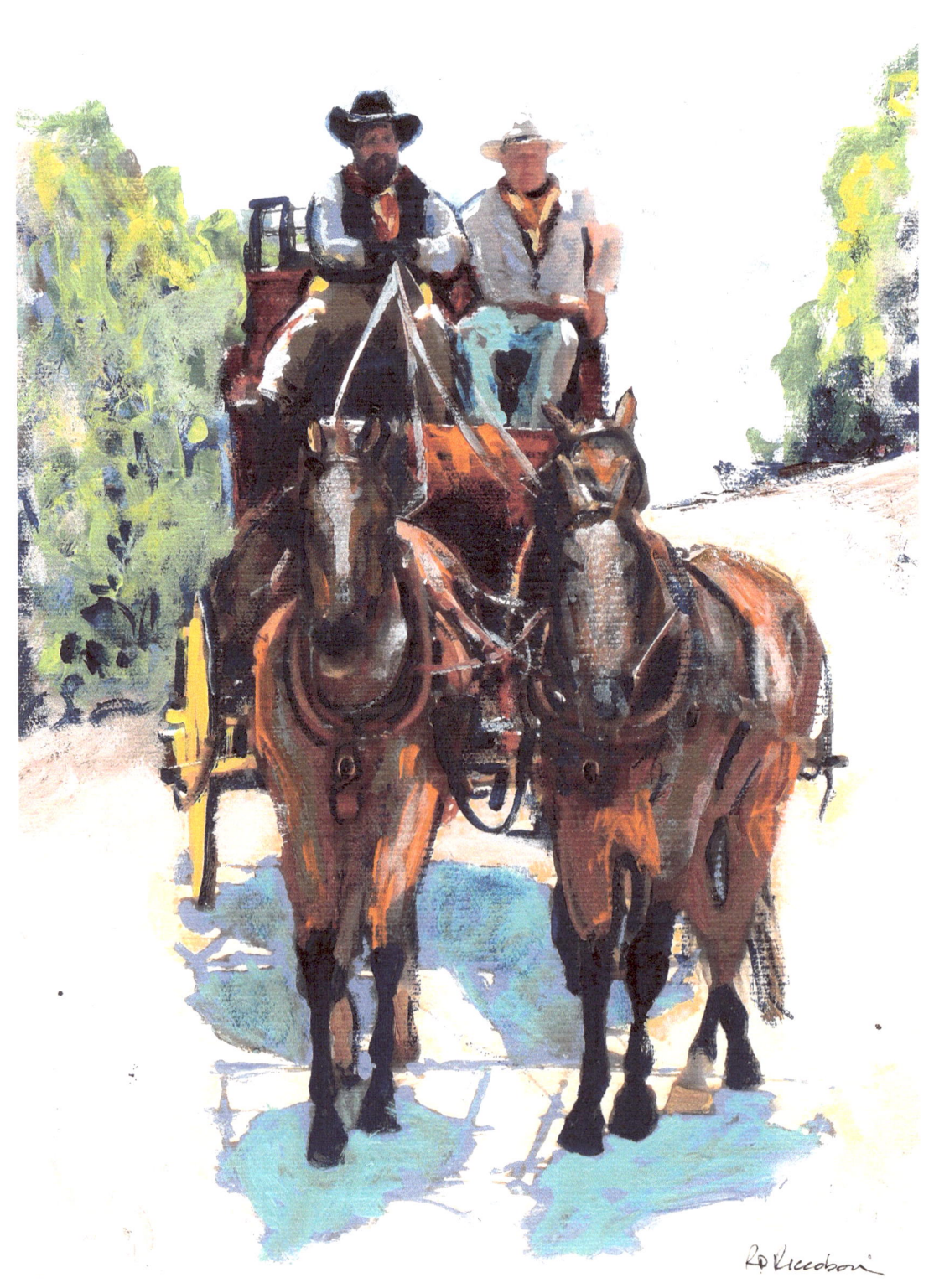

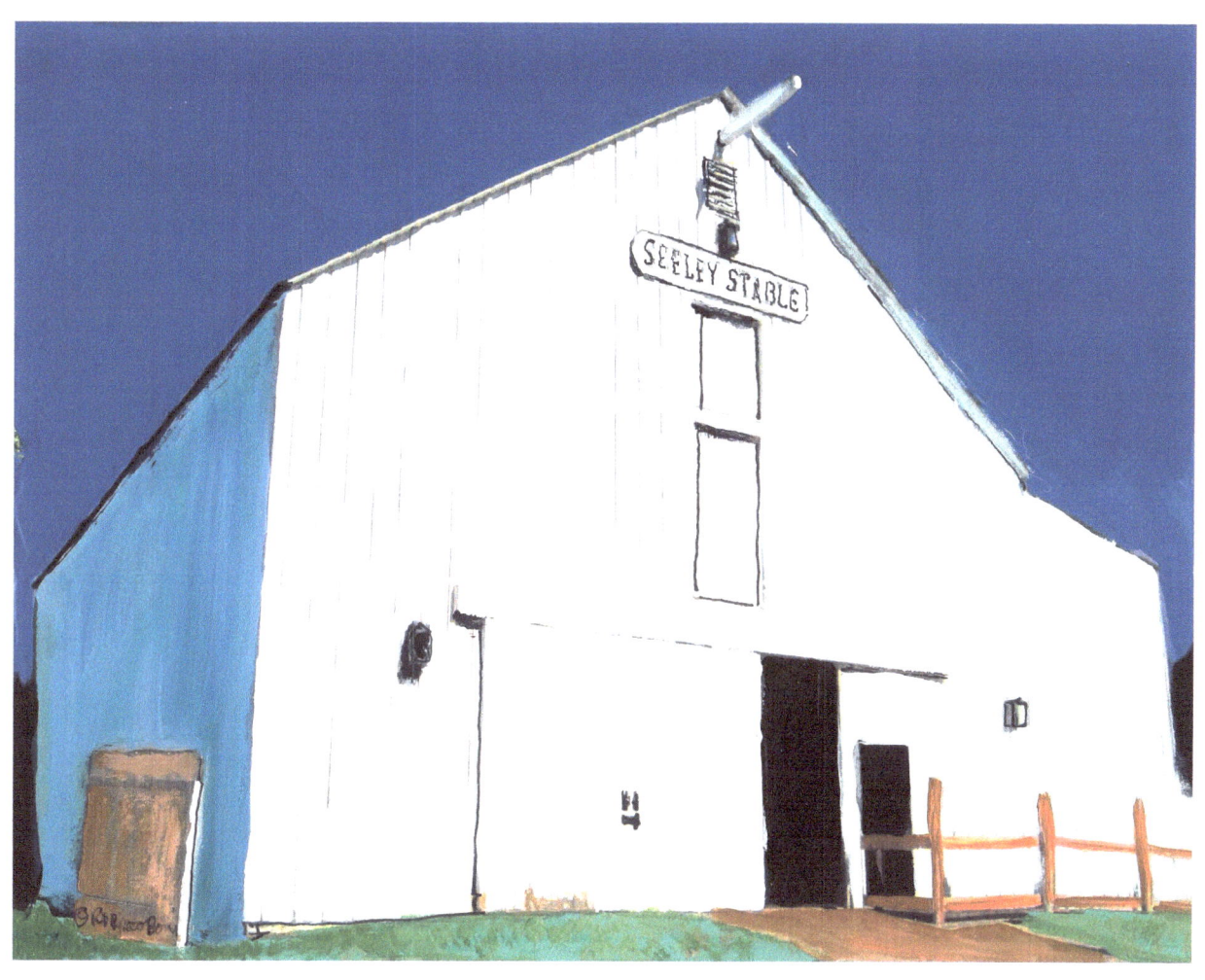

Left: *The San Diego Stage comes to Town*.

Above; *The Seeley Stables*

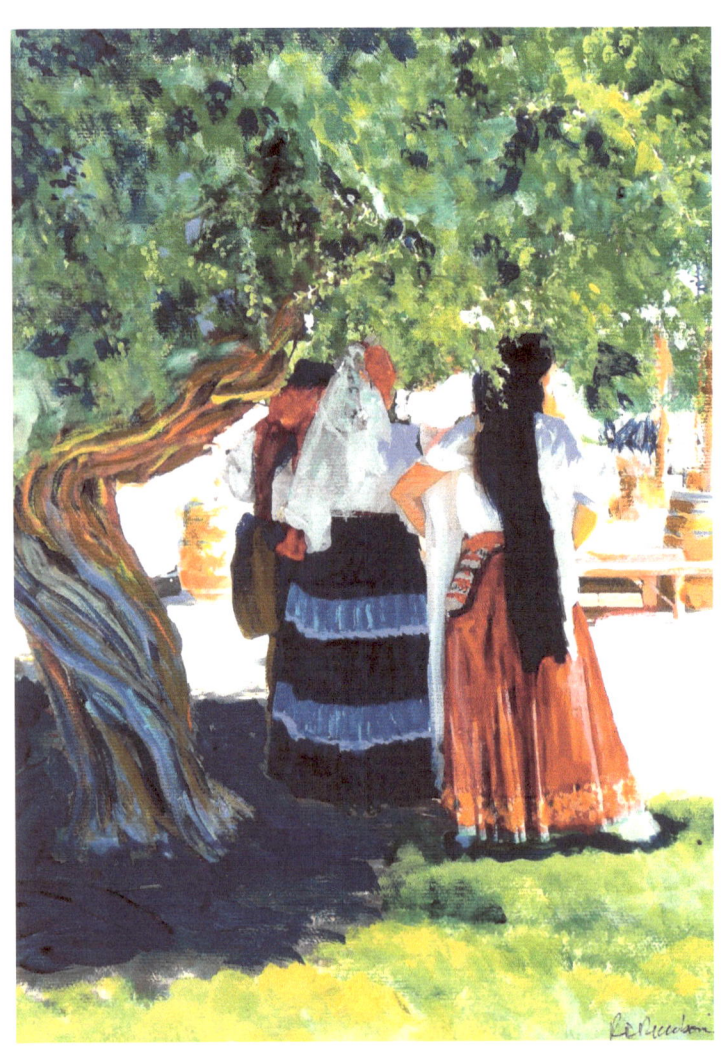

Reteat from the Noonday Sun
Old Town, San Diego

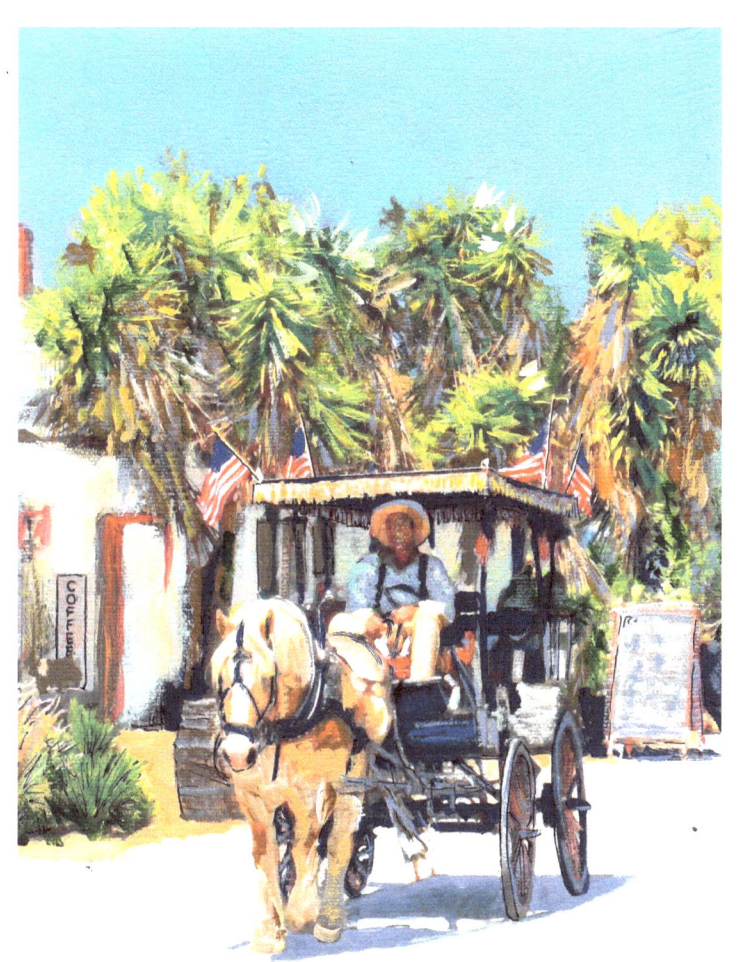

R. Buccoleni

Holiday Ride in Old Town San Diego

Old Buggy
in Old Town Town San Diego State Historic
Park

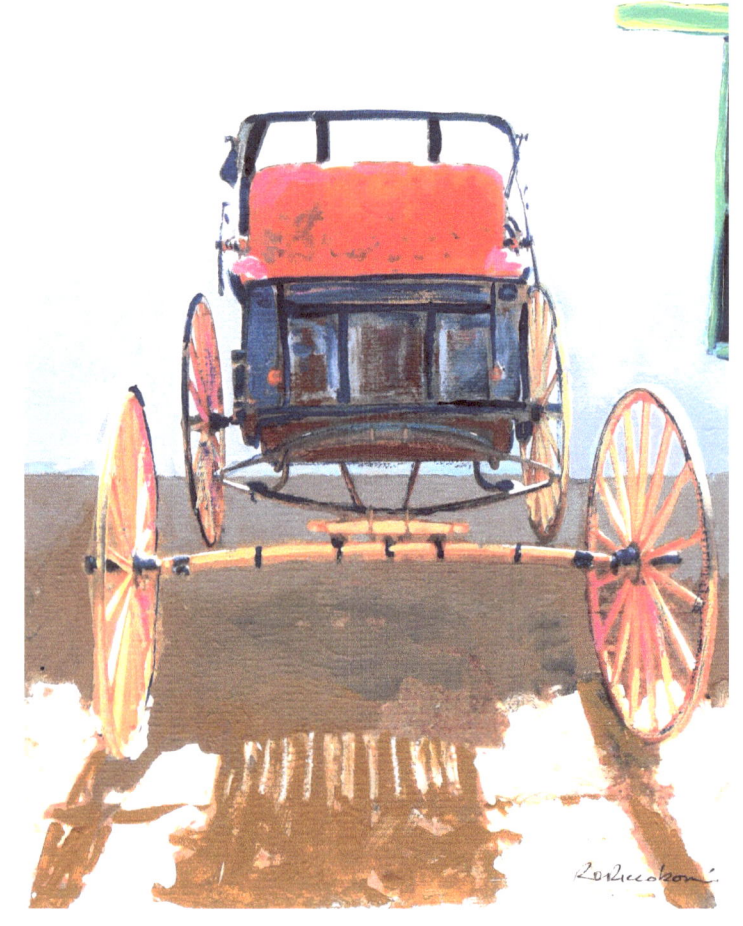

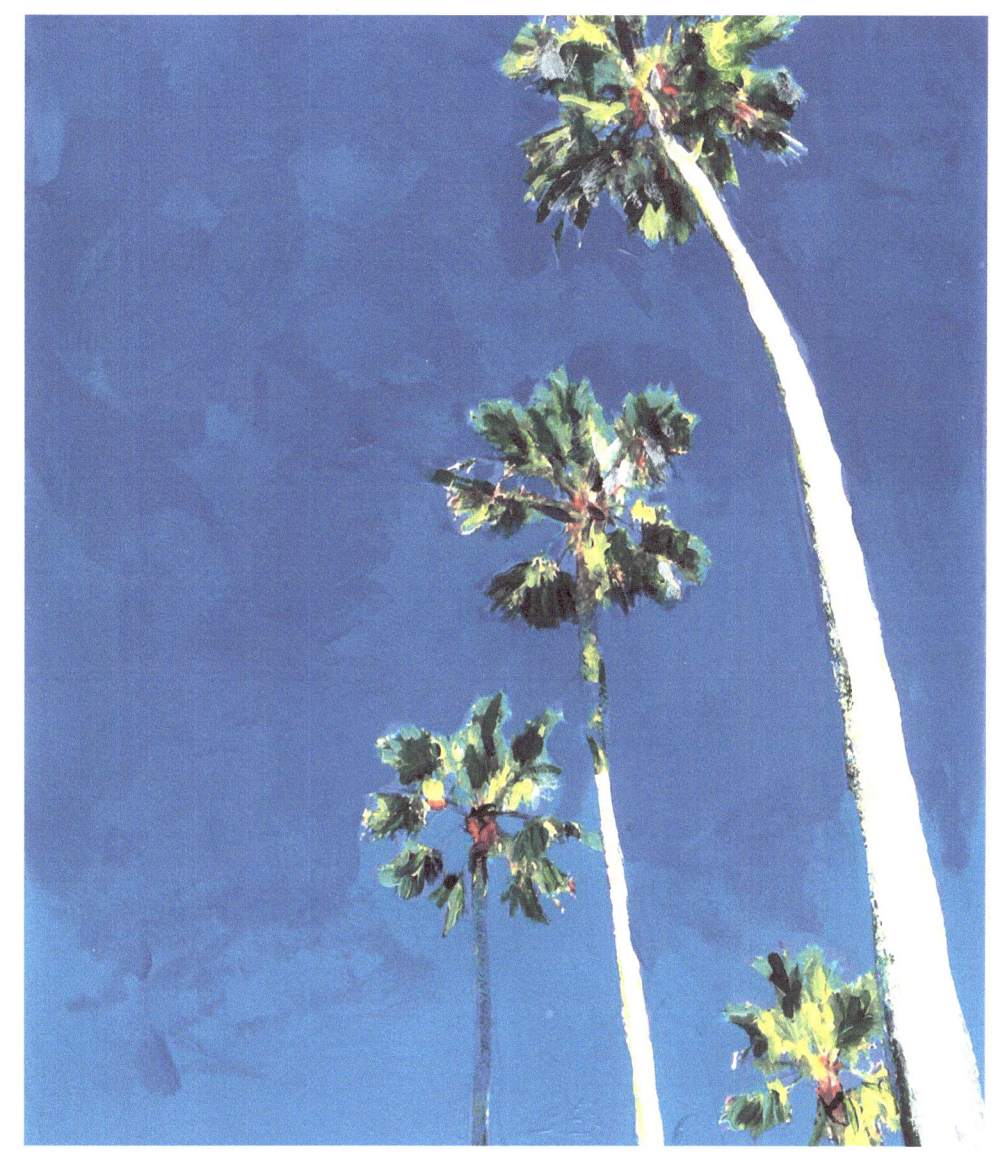

A Little Piece of Heaven

These palm trees are at Swami's beach in Encinitas California. This painting is also featured on the cover of Manifest Success Volume 2, Miracles,Movtivation and Motivation. By Deborah L. Chambers and features a story about Riccoboni and how one his first shows came about.

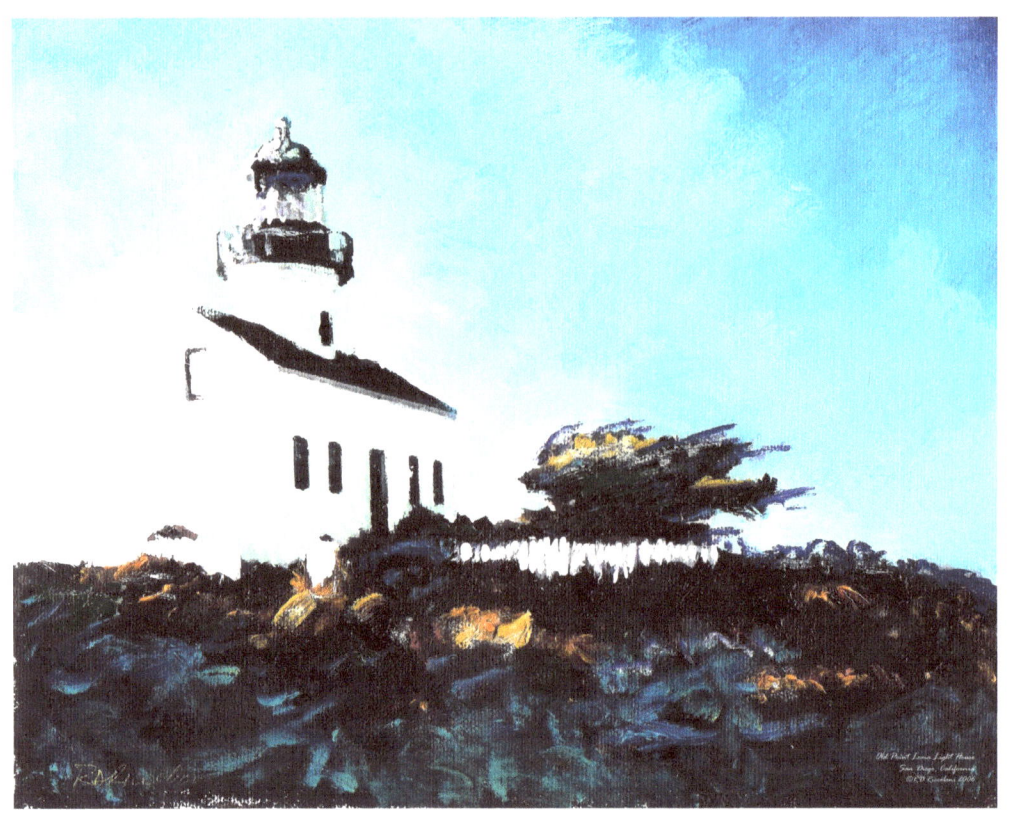

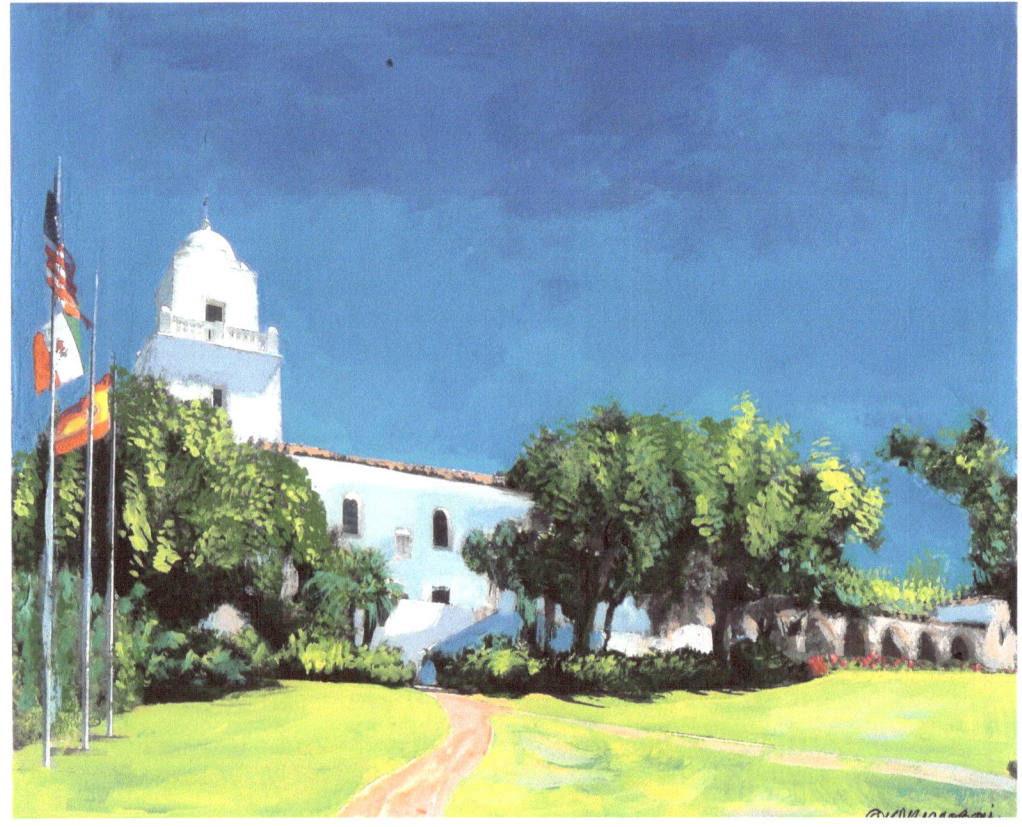

Above: **Old Point Loma Lighthouse** at Cabrillo National
Monument
Below: The **Serra Museum at Presidio Park** - Old Town

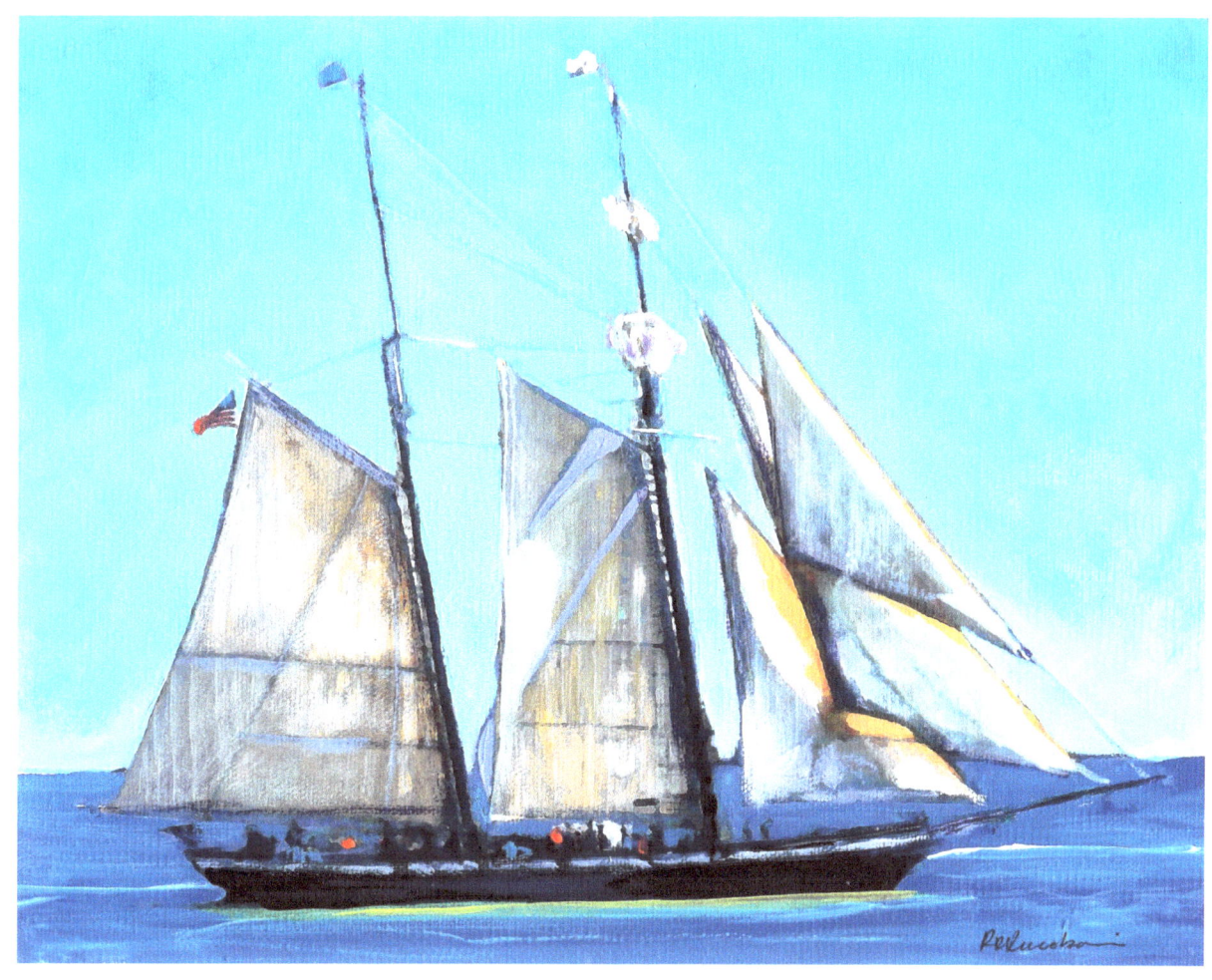

The Californian

The Tallship Californian is a replica of the 1847
Revenue Cutter C.W. Lawrence, that patrolled
the coast of California enforcing federal law
during the gold rush.

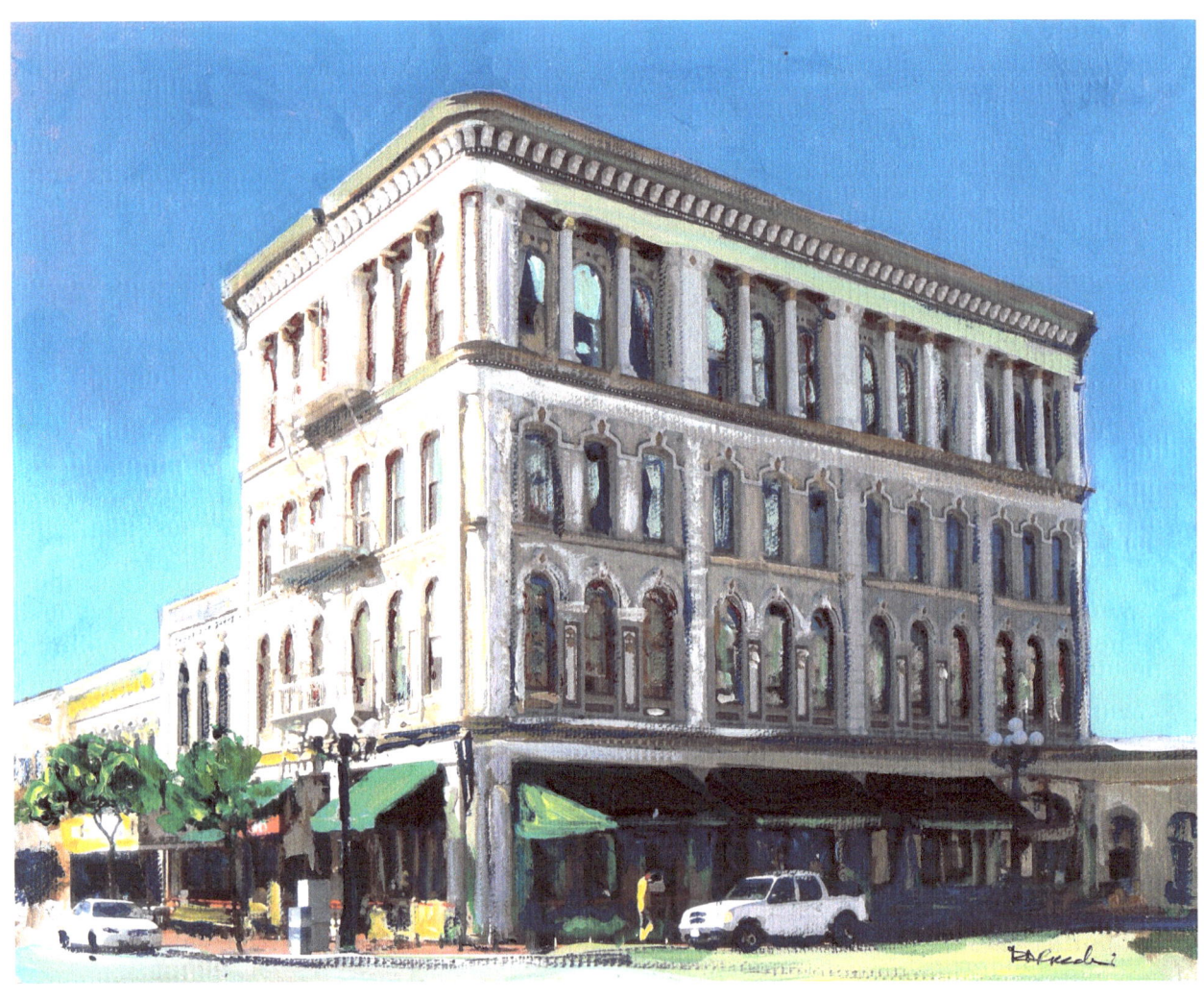

Old San Diego City Hall

The Gaslamp district, Downtown San Diego
California.

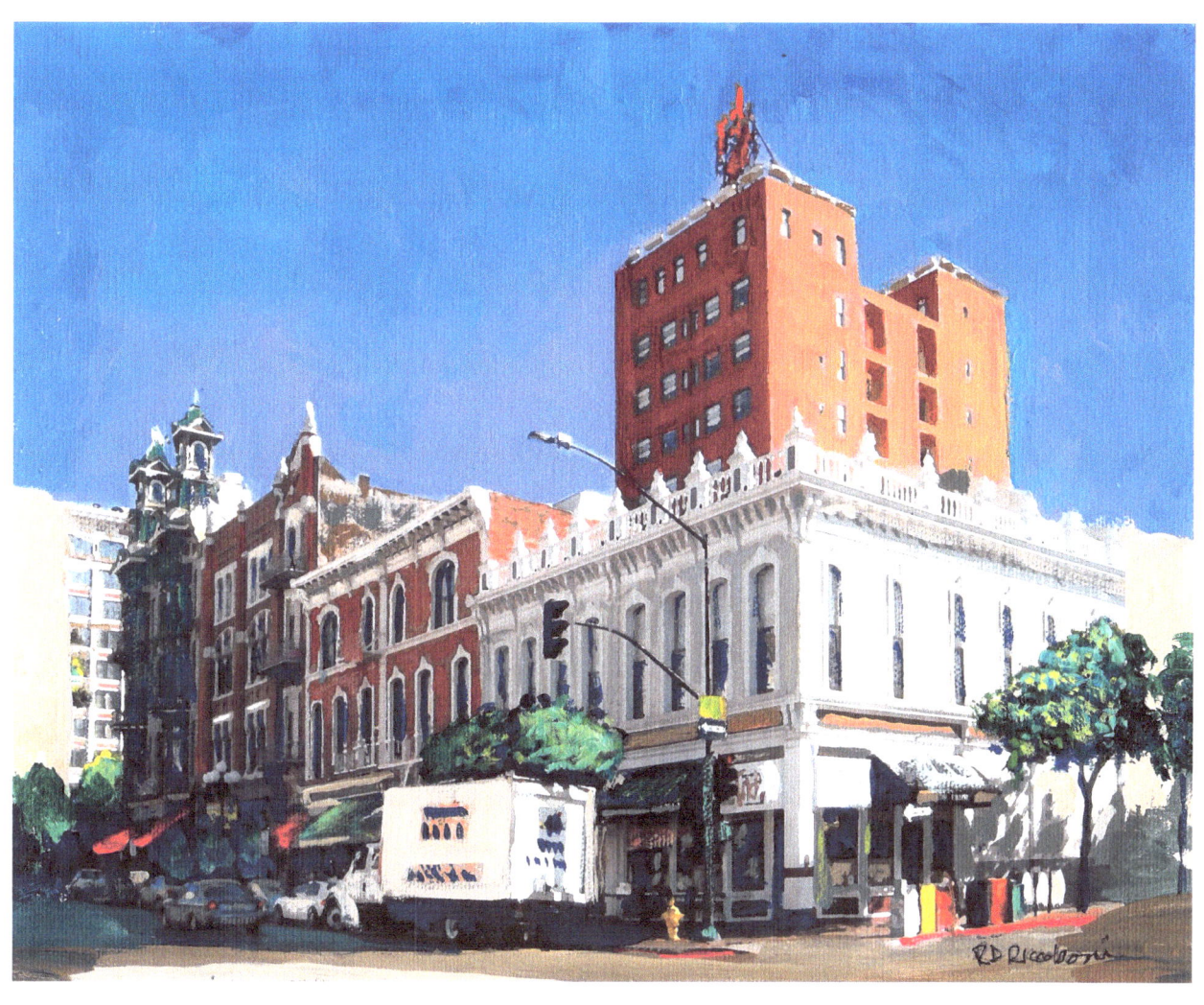

Marston Block San Diego
The Gaslamp district, Downtown San Diego
California.

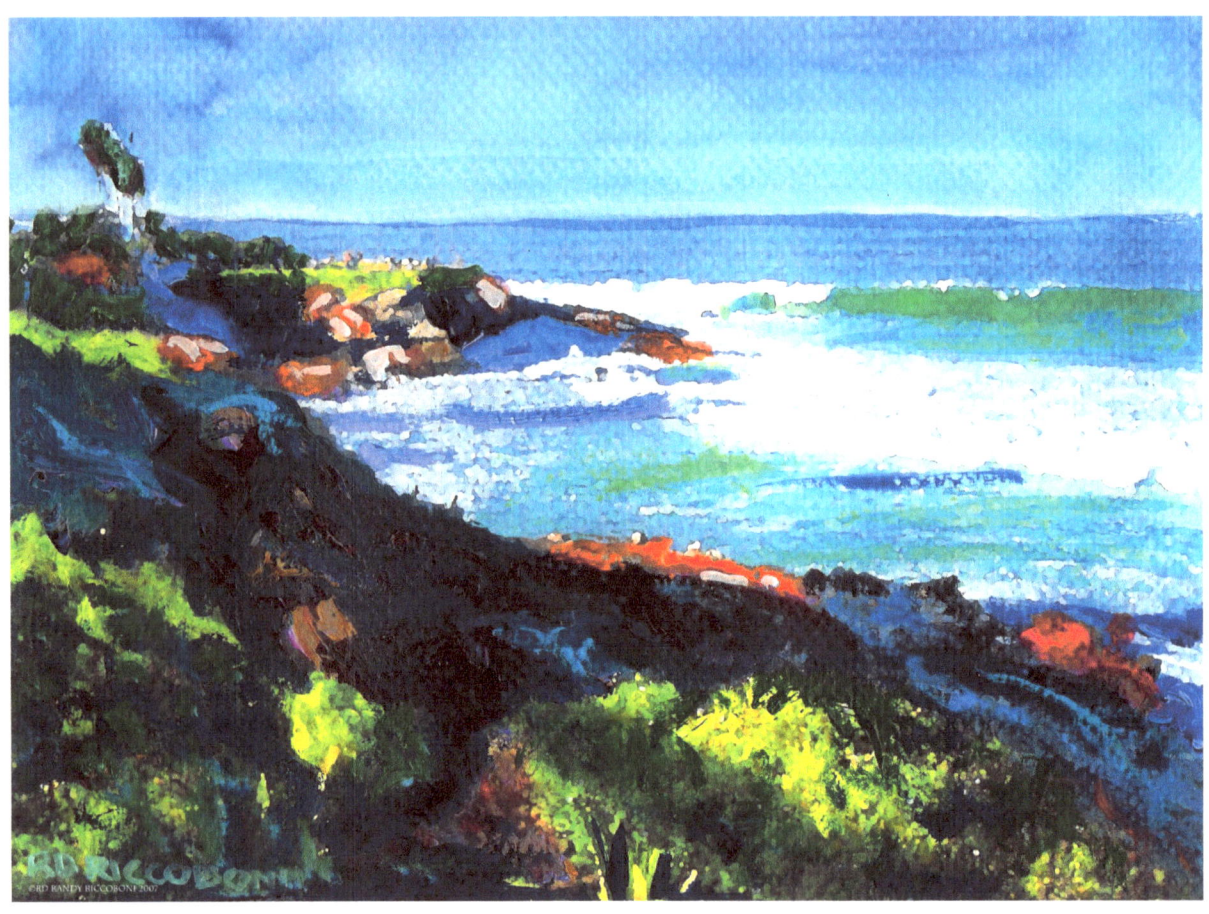

West to The Pacific.

La Jolla Cove San Diego, Califonia. La Jolla Cove
is a very small beach, tucked between adjacent
sandstone cliffs. Due to its extraordinary
beauty, La Jolla Cove is one of the most
photographed beaches in Southern California.
It is within a short walk of the commercial area
of the community of La Jolla, but retains a
character all its own.

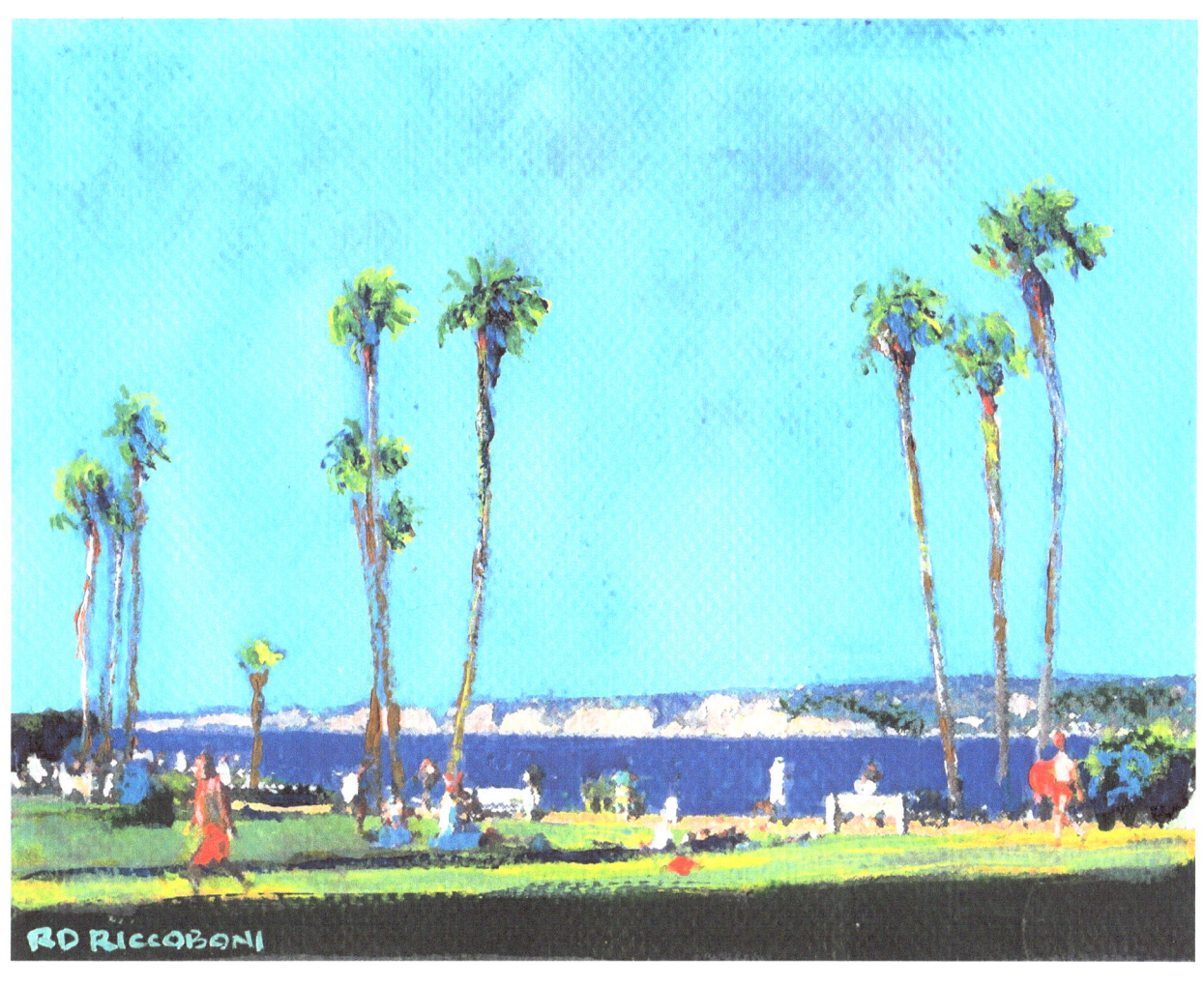

Scripps Park La Jolla Cove

This is Scripps Park above La Jolla Cove in san Diego. The park above is the beach. I have painted this area many times. This view looks northward acros the cove towards the cliffs above Black's Beach.

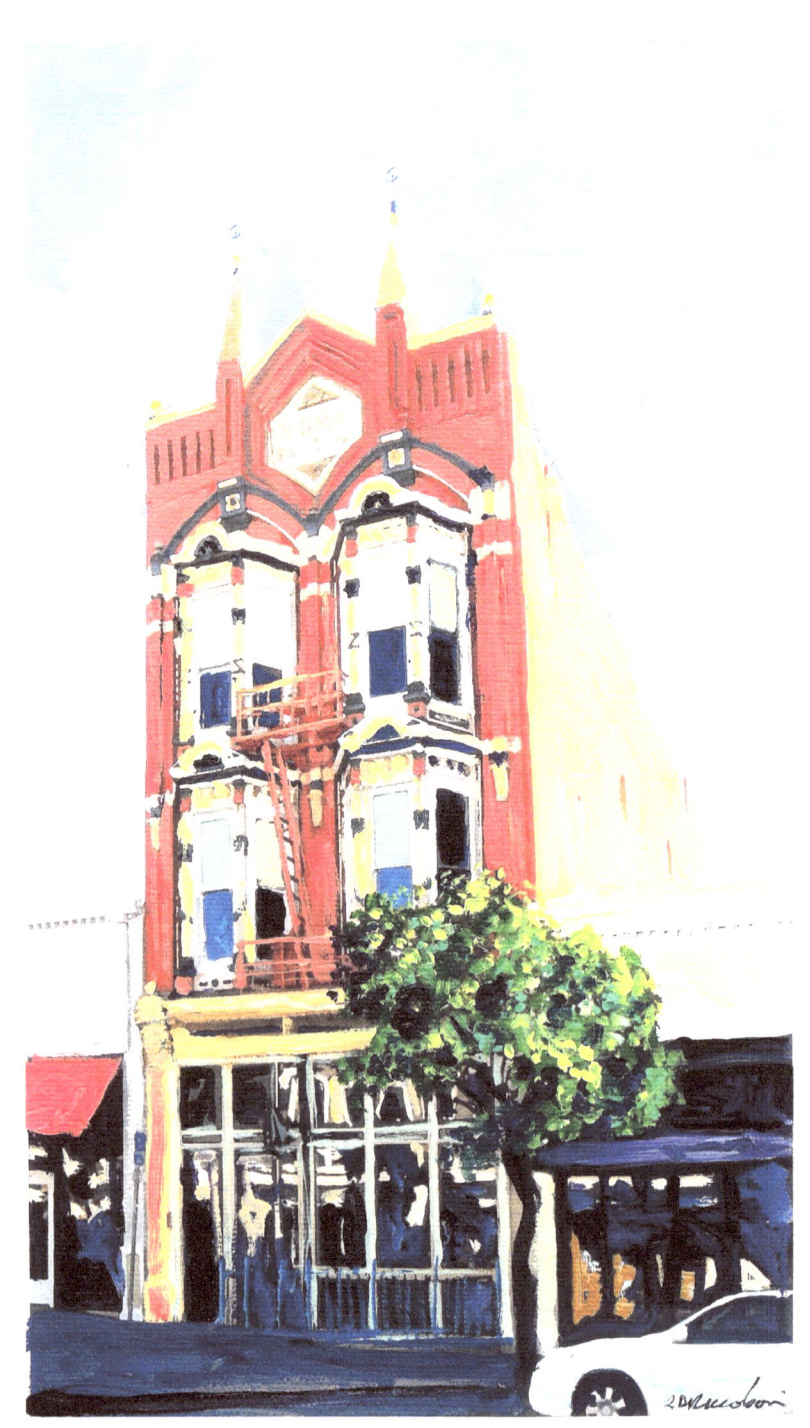

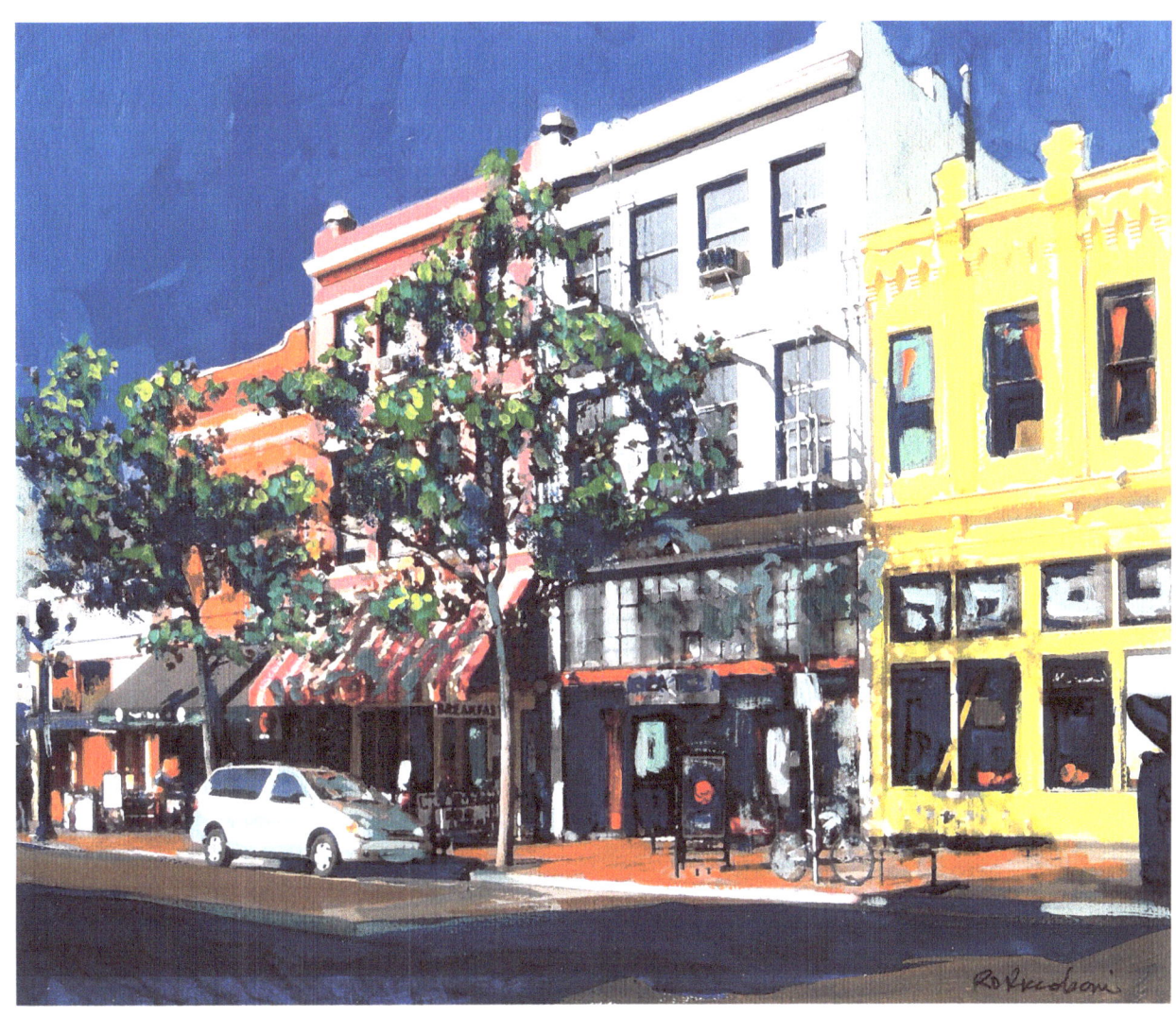

The historic Gaslamp district, Downtown San Diego California.

Left, *The Yuma Building*

Top, *Fifth Avenue*

The historic Loring, Fritz and Spencer Ogden / DeLeval buildings on Fifth Avenue.

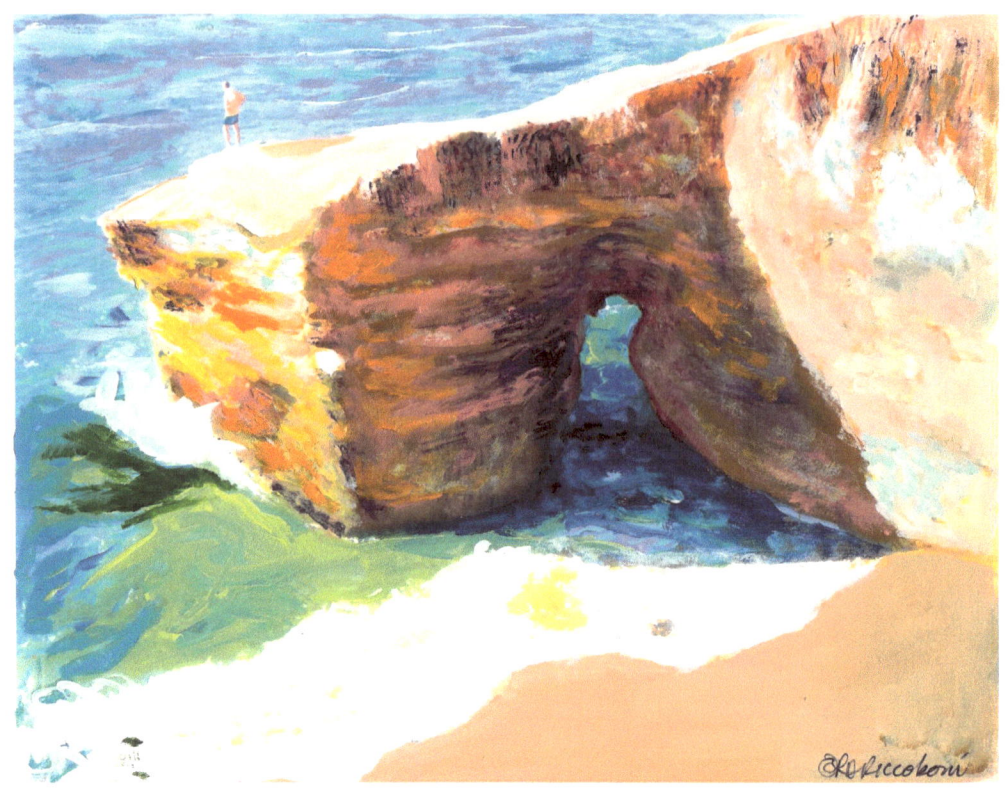

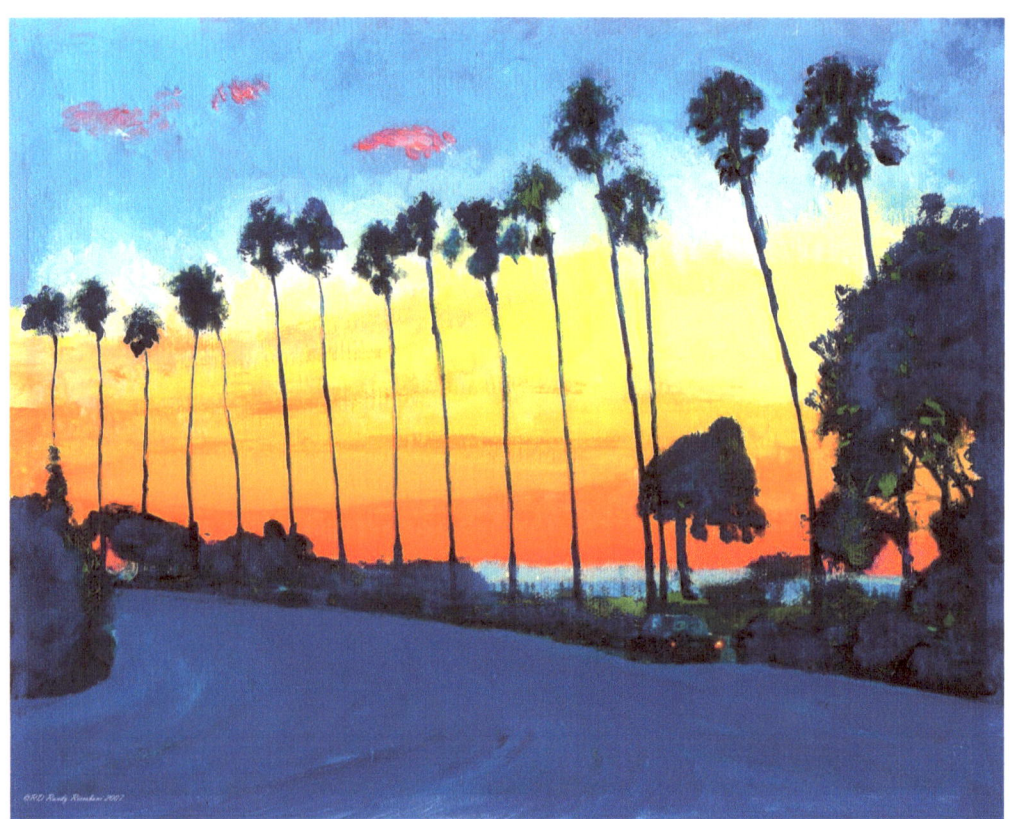

Above: ***Arch at Sunset Cliffs***, Point Loma
Below: ***California Sunset*** - La Jolla Cove

Page Right: ***Sunset Over Texas Street Canyon*** University Heights

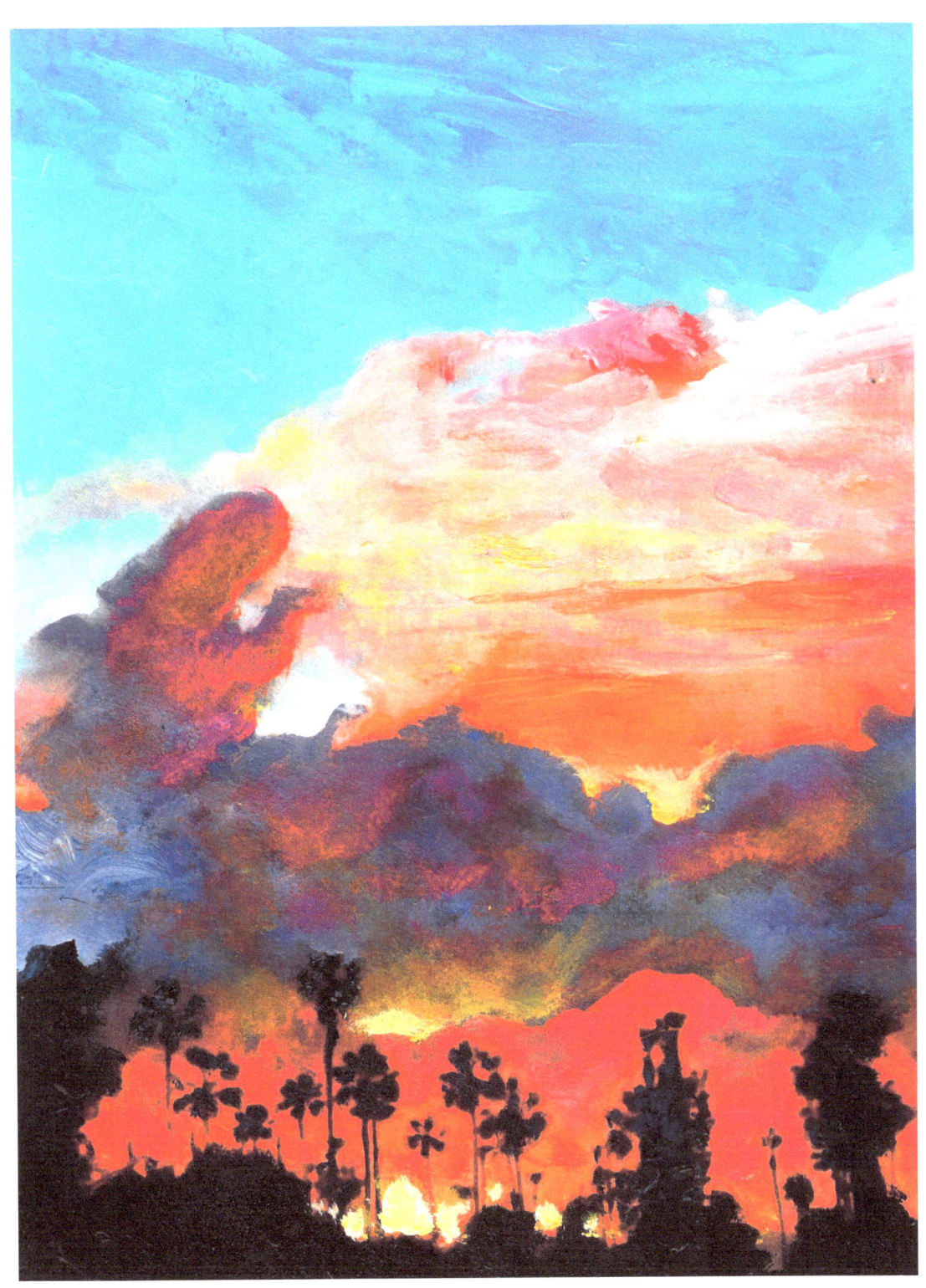

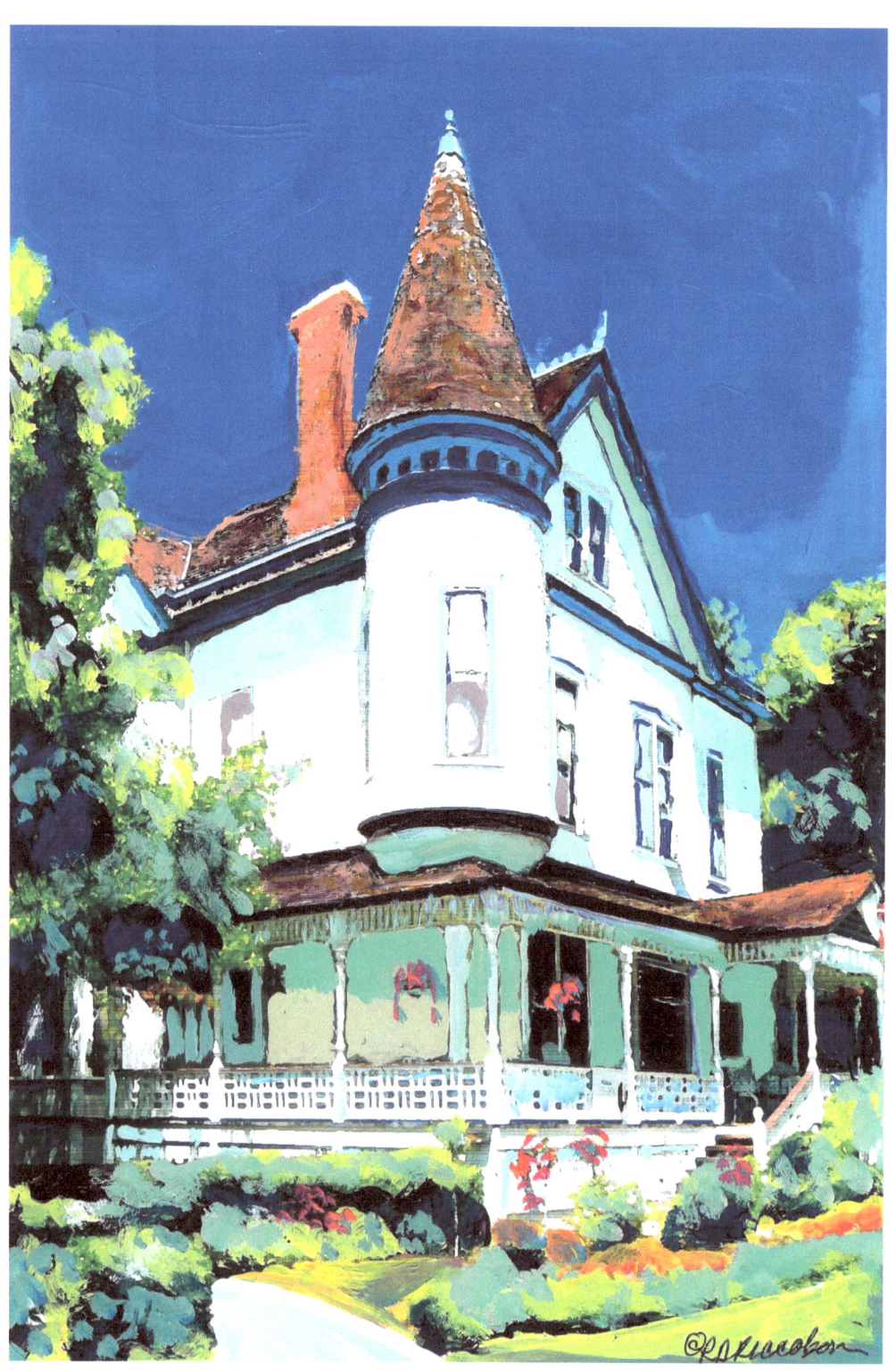

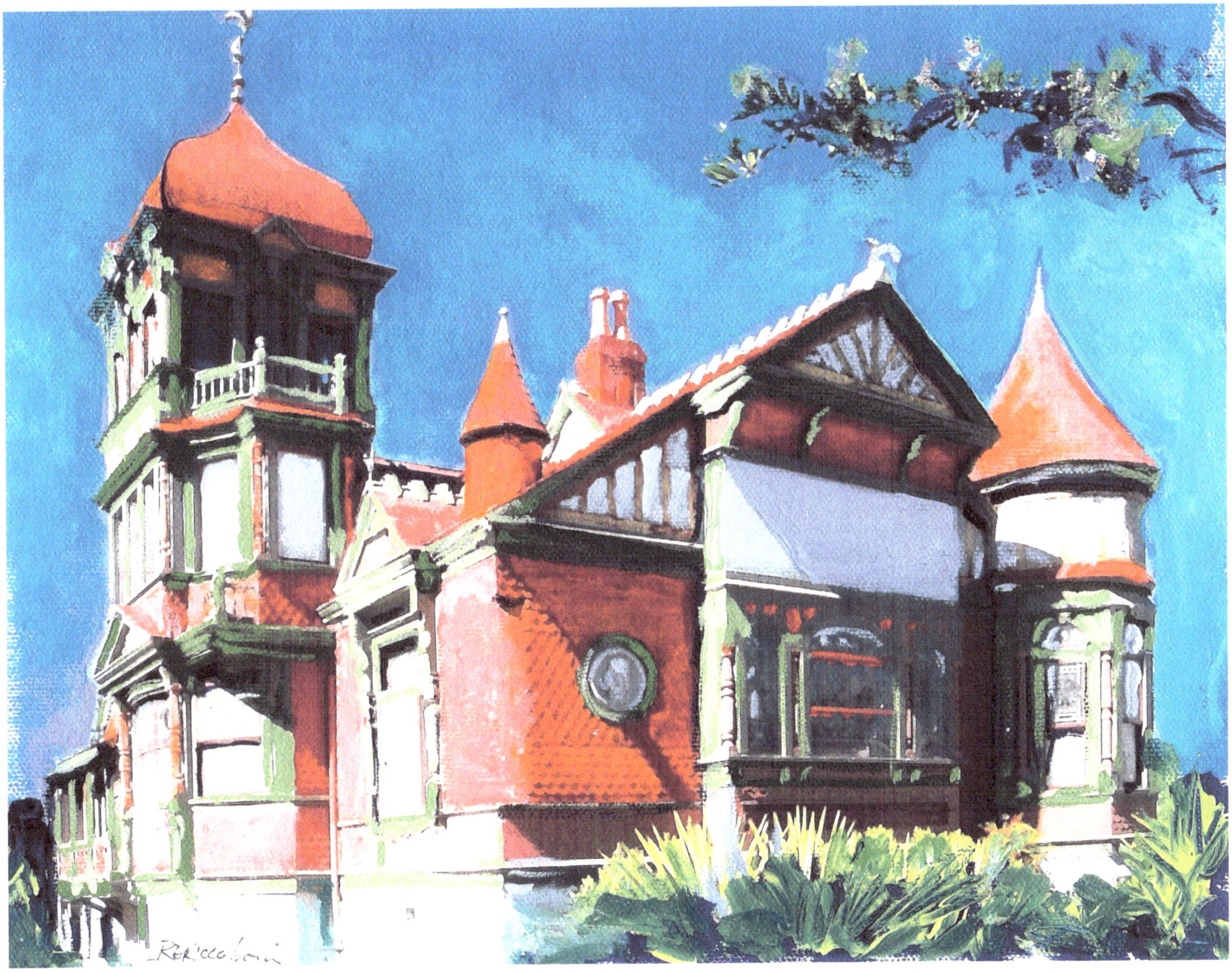

Page Left: **The Christian House**
Old Town San Diego

Above: ***Villa Montezuma*** - Sherman
Heights

Right: ***The San Diego Gaslamp***
downtown

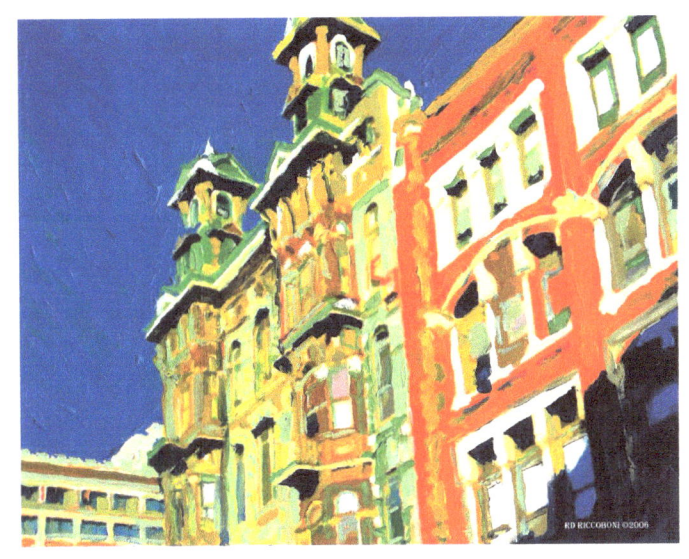

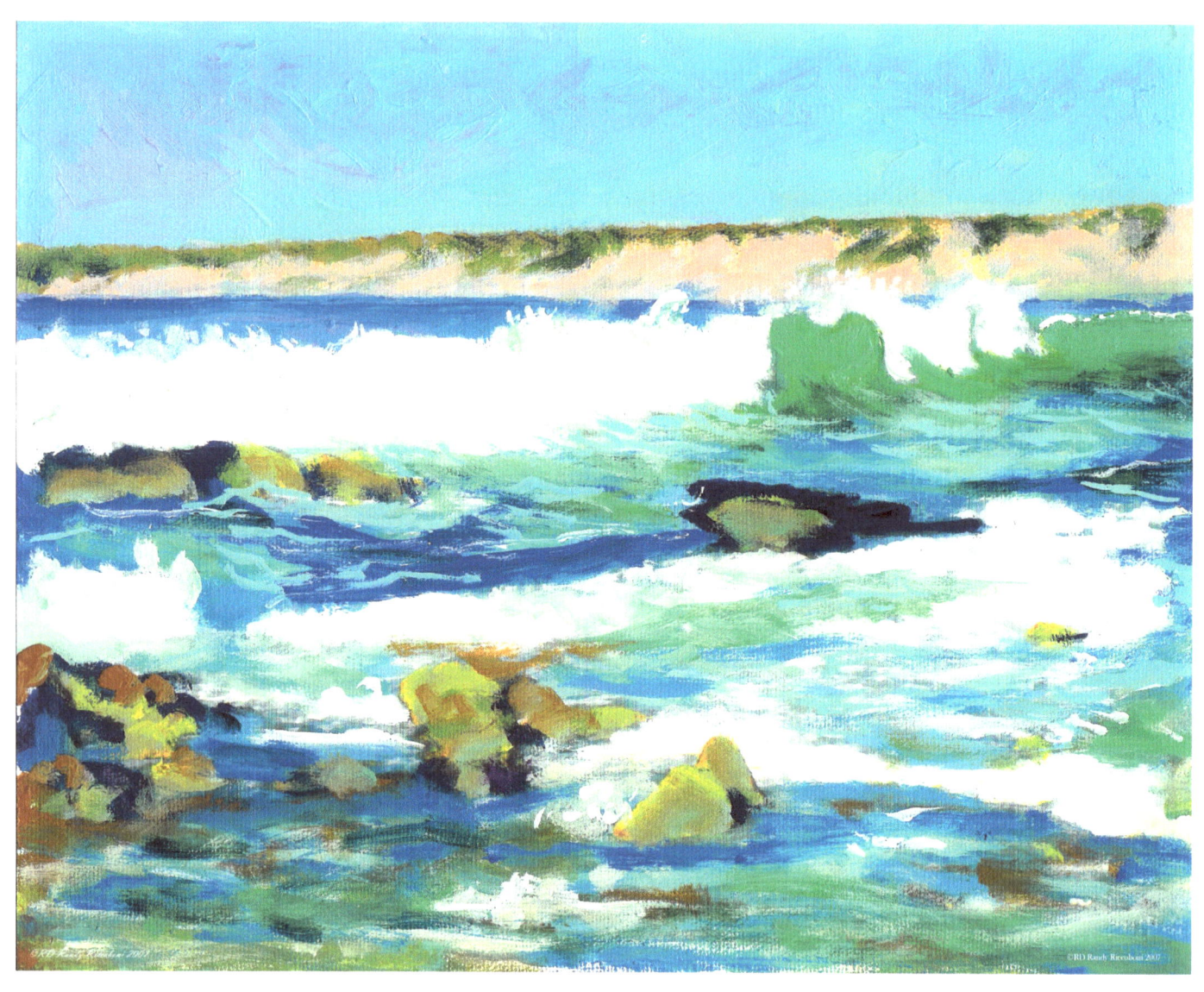

Above: **Waves in La Jolla Cove,**

Following page, top; **Calm Sea in La Jolla Cove**
Bottom Left: **San Diego Harbor Sunset.**
San Diego bay and Maritme Center, HMS Surprise.

Bottom Right: **Picnic in Scripps Park La Jolla Cove**
La Jolla

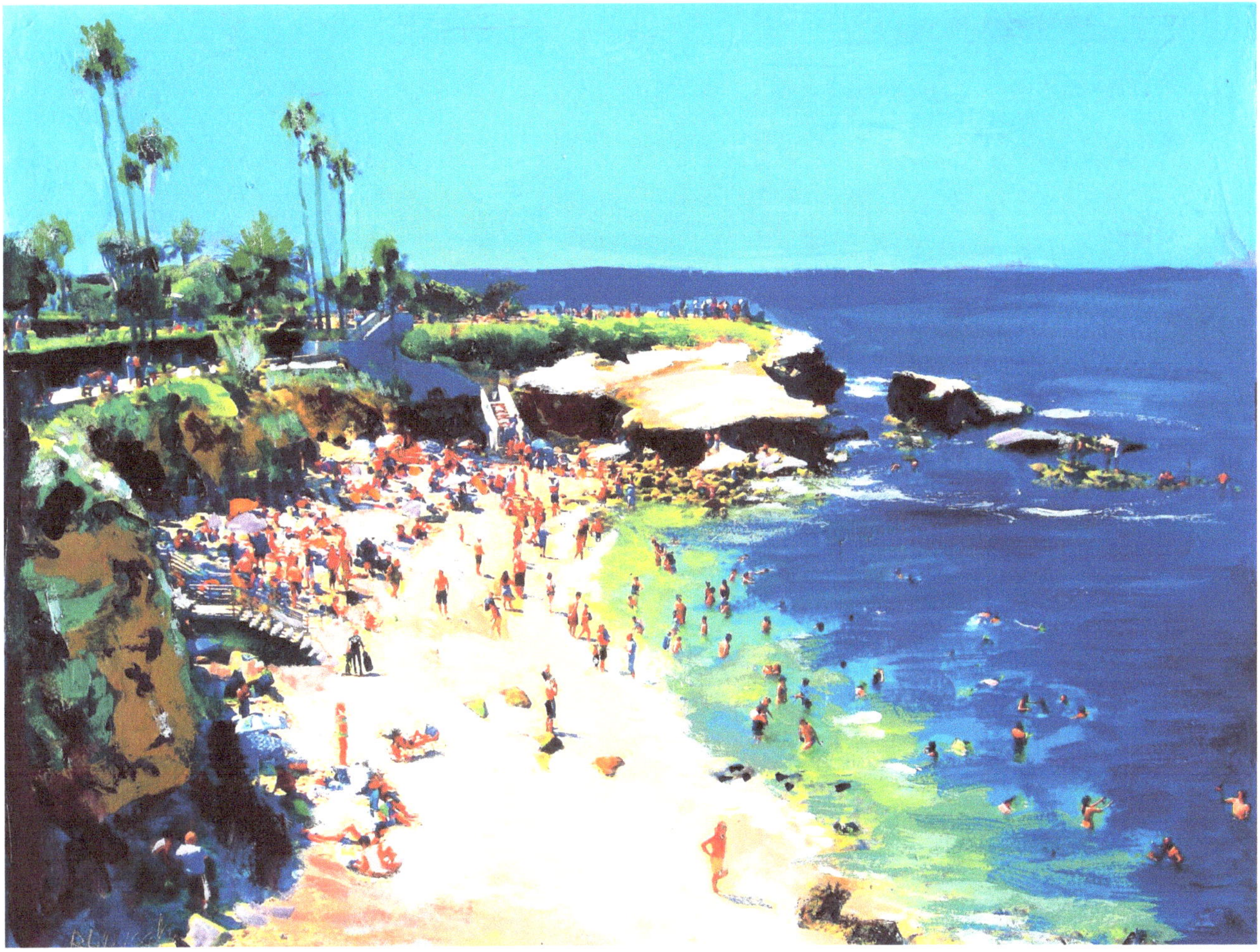

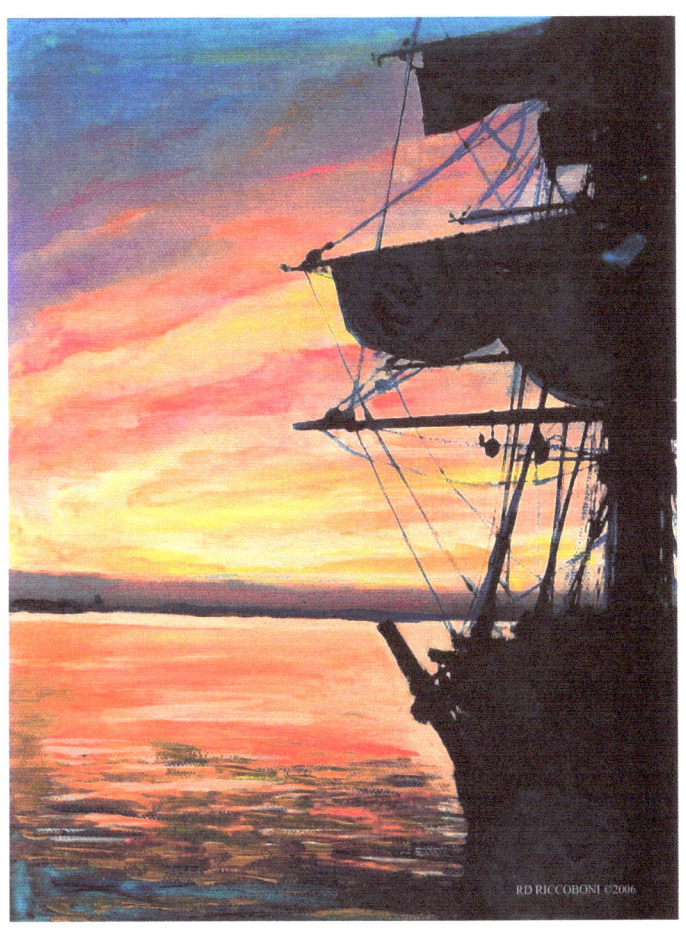

San Diego Harbor Sunset

Cornado

Left: *Hotel del Coronado from the Beach*

Following page right: *Coronado Beach*

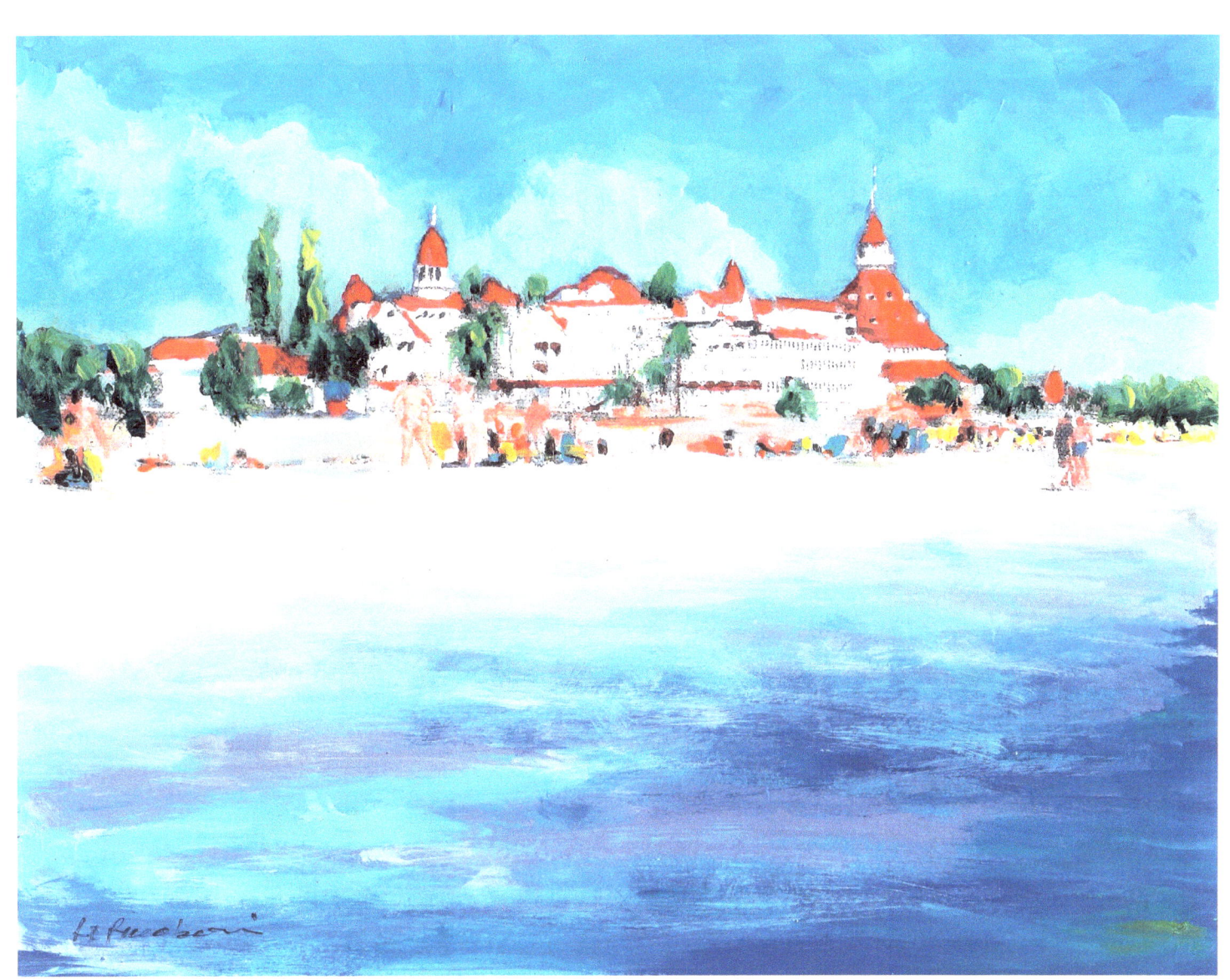

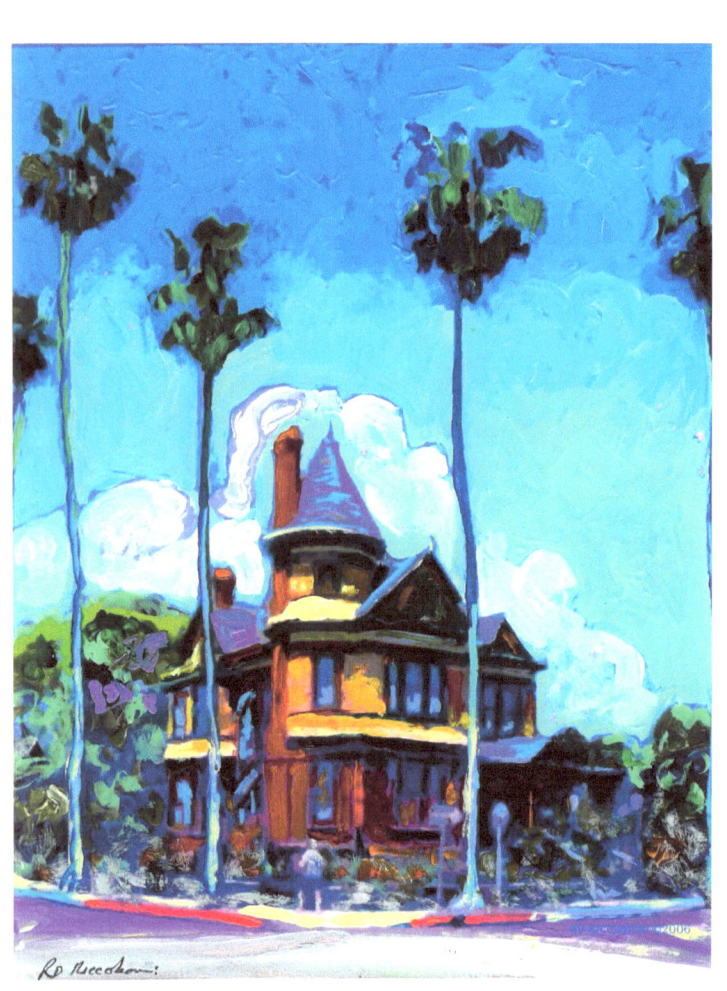

Around Balboa Park

Left: **The Britt Scripps House**, Bankers Hill

Right: **The Calfornia Bell Tower**
Balboa Park

Following pages: Balboa Park
Casa Del Prado - The Childrens Theater

Casa Del Prado Courtyard

Botanical Building and Reflecting Pool

**Two Towers in The Park
and Reflecting Pool**

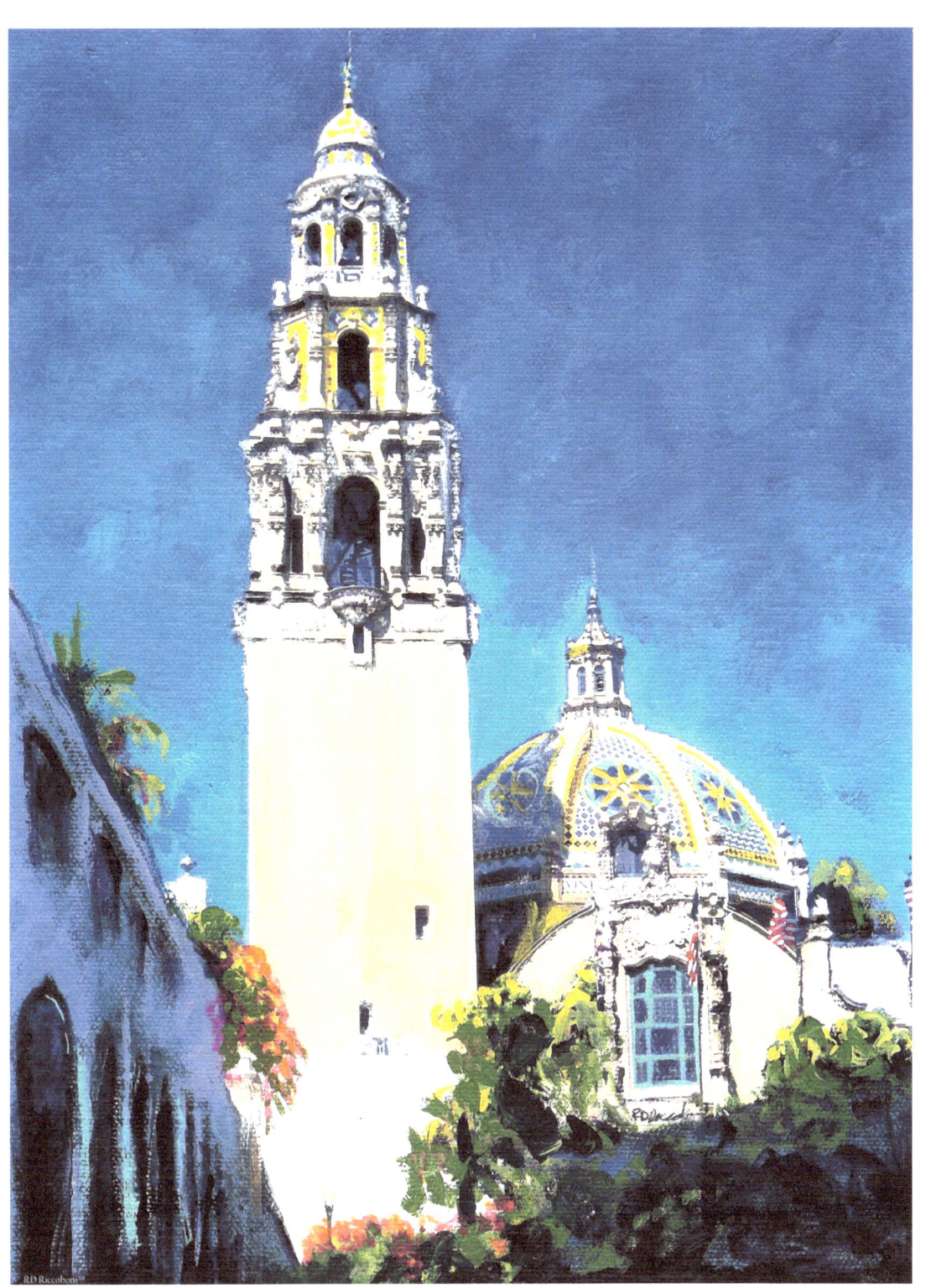

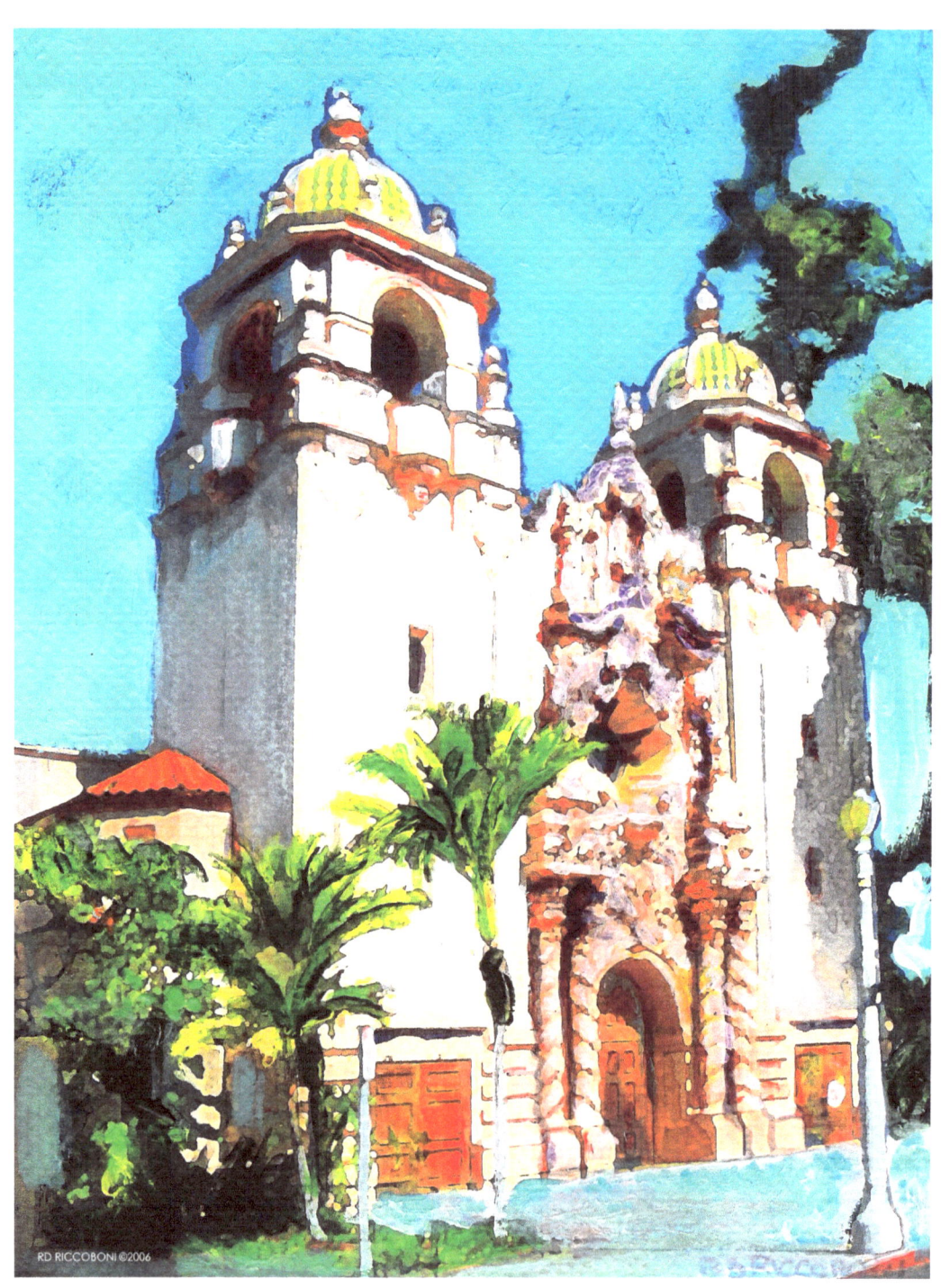

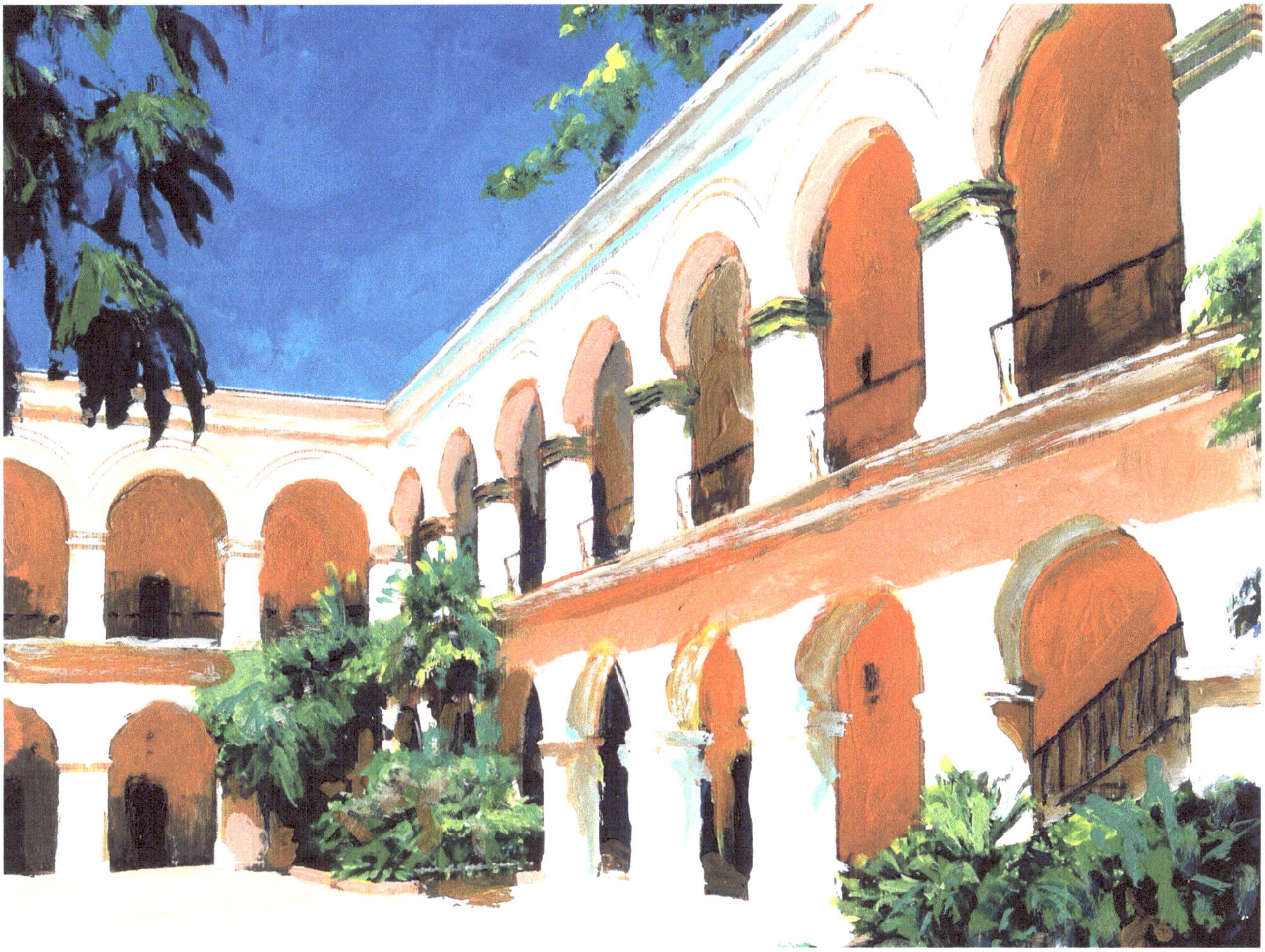

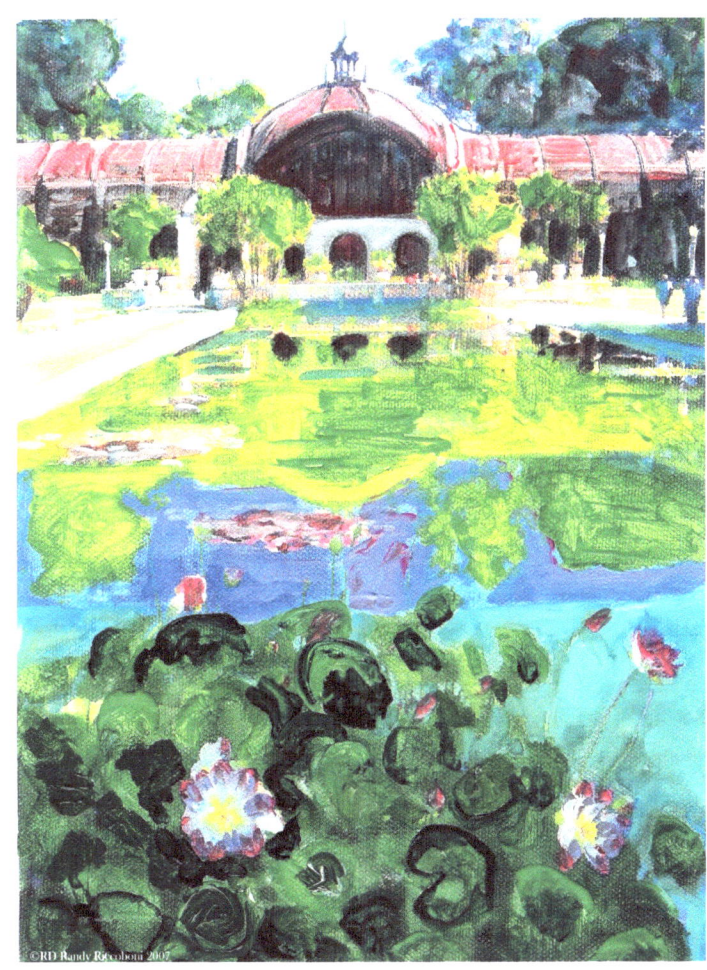

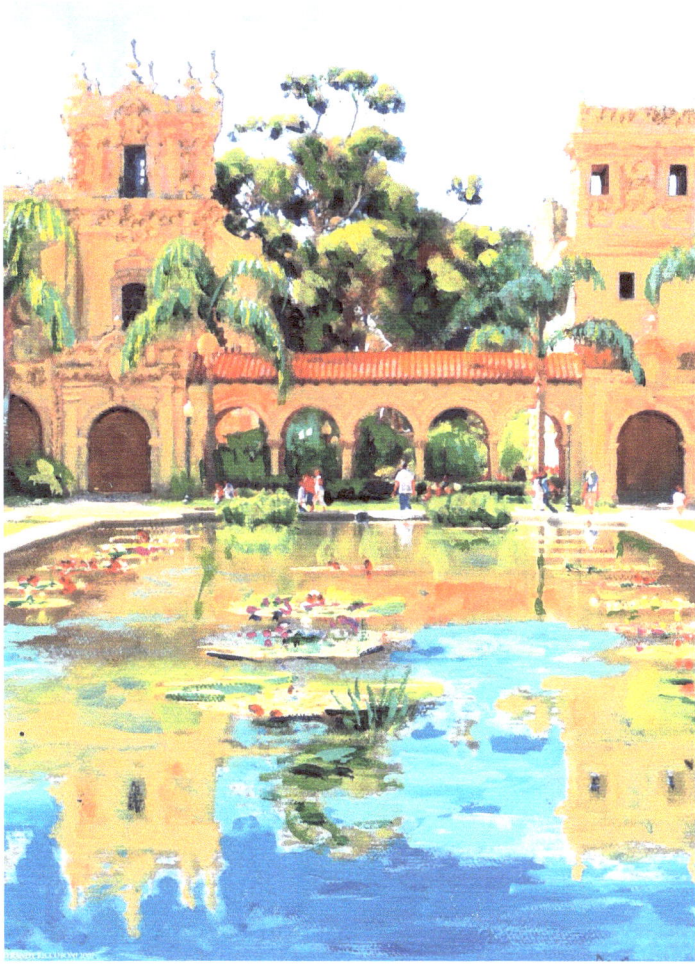

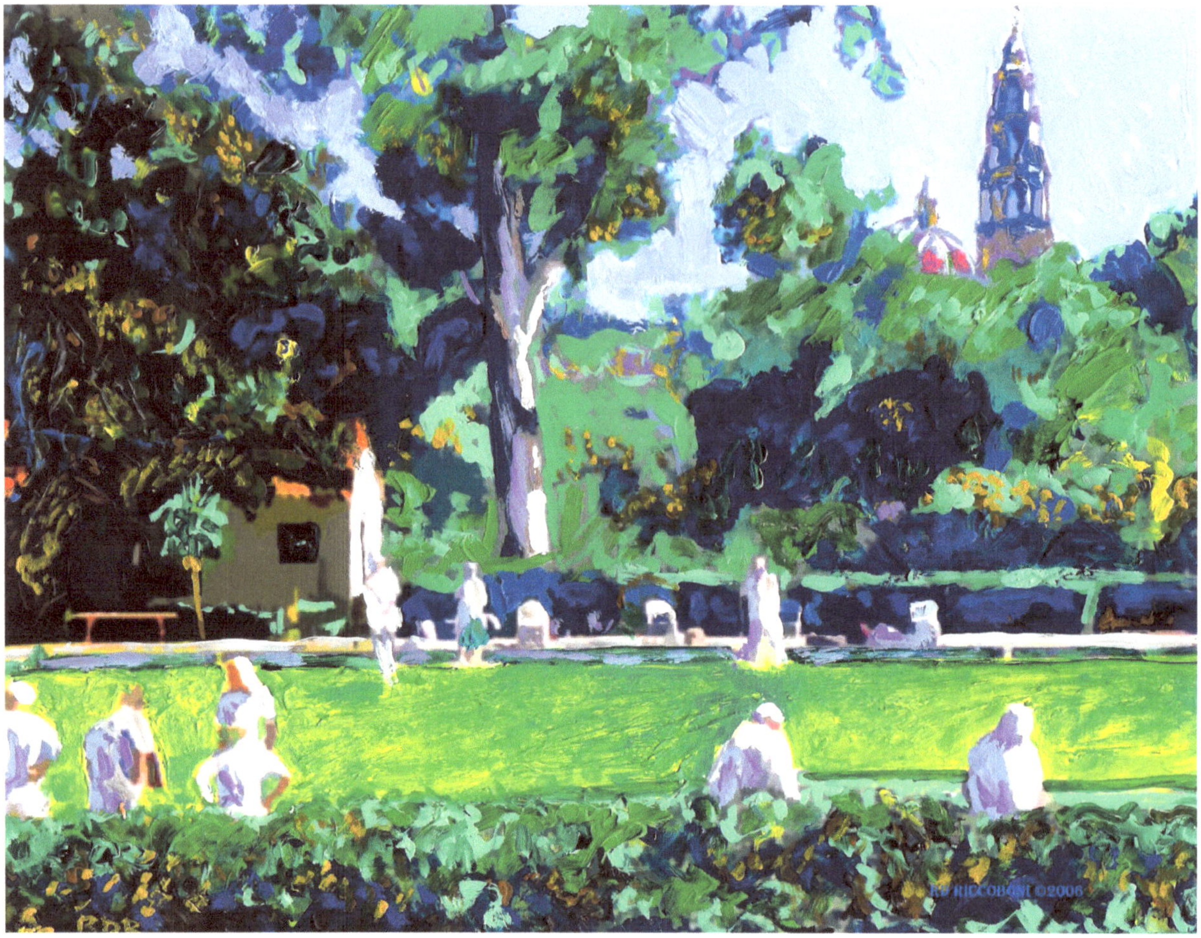

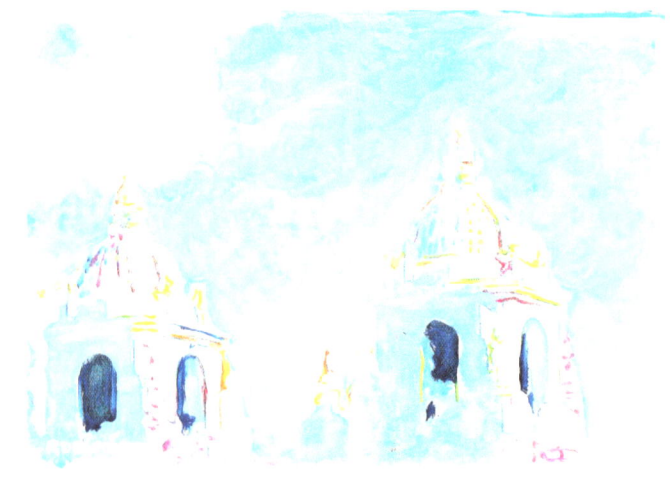

Top: ***The Lawn Bowlers in Balboa Park***
Right: ***Spires In the Park*** - Casa Del Prado

Following page:
Left: ***Balboa Park at Night***
Right: ***Big Tree in The Park***

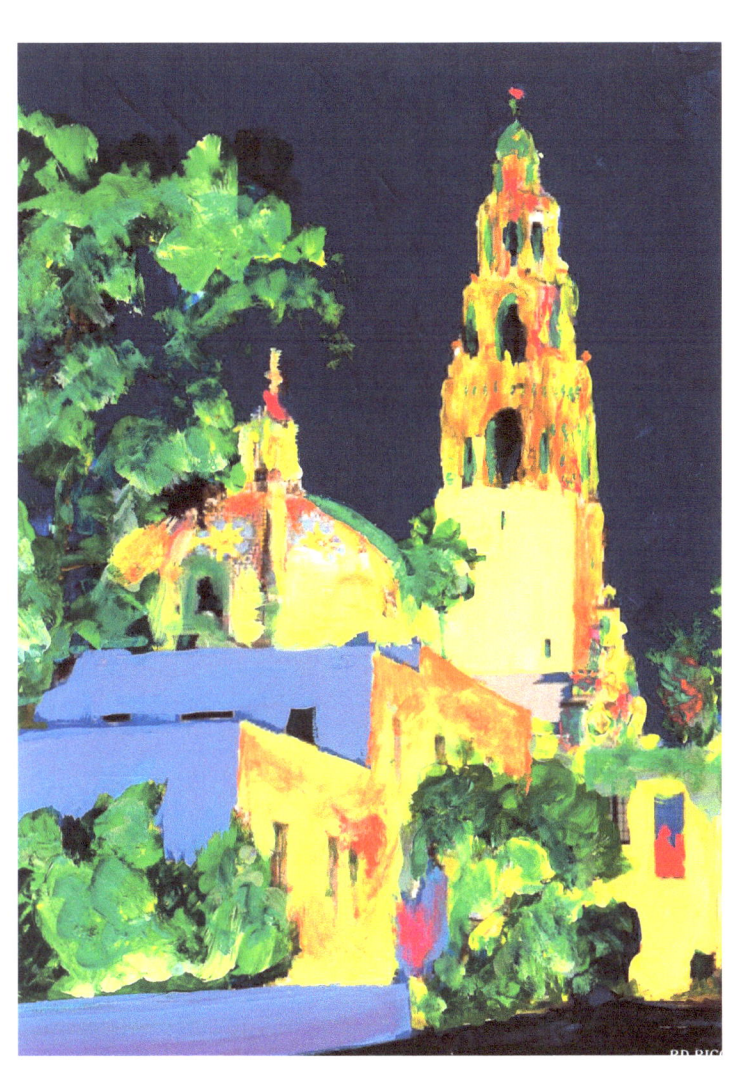 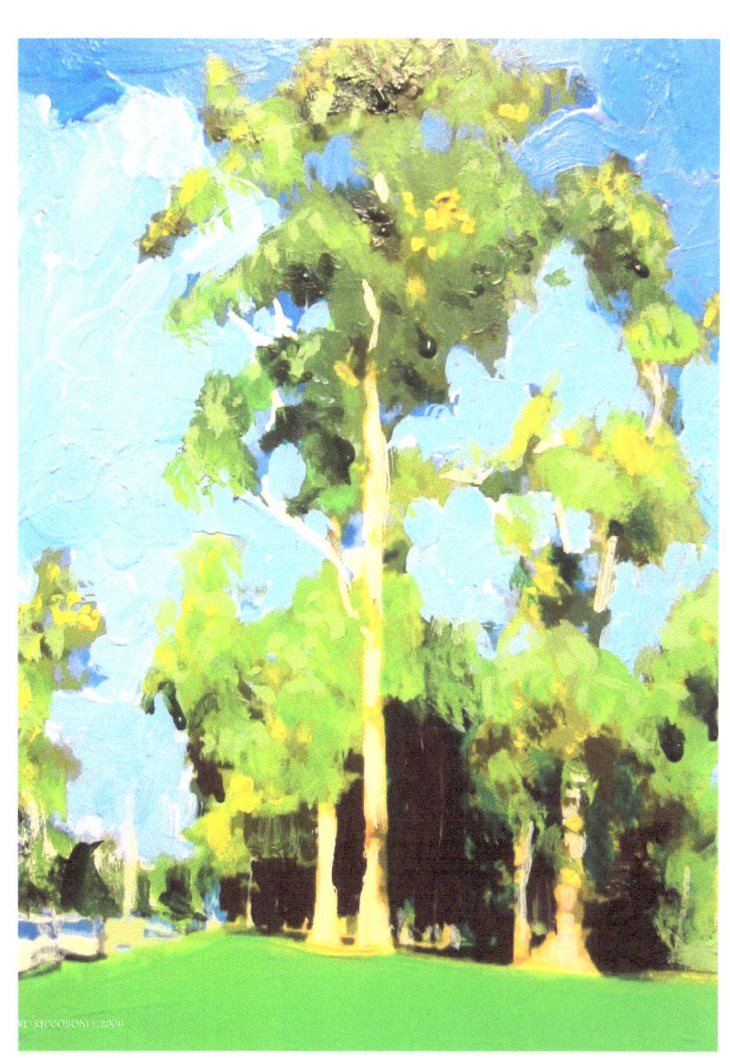

Field Trip to Balboa Park

Following Page: Arches in Balboa Park

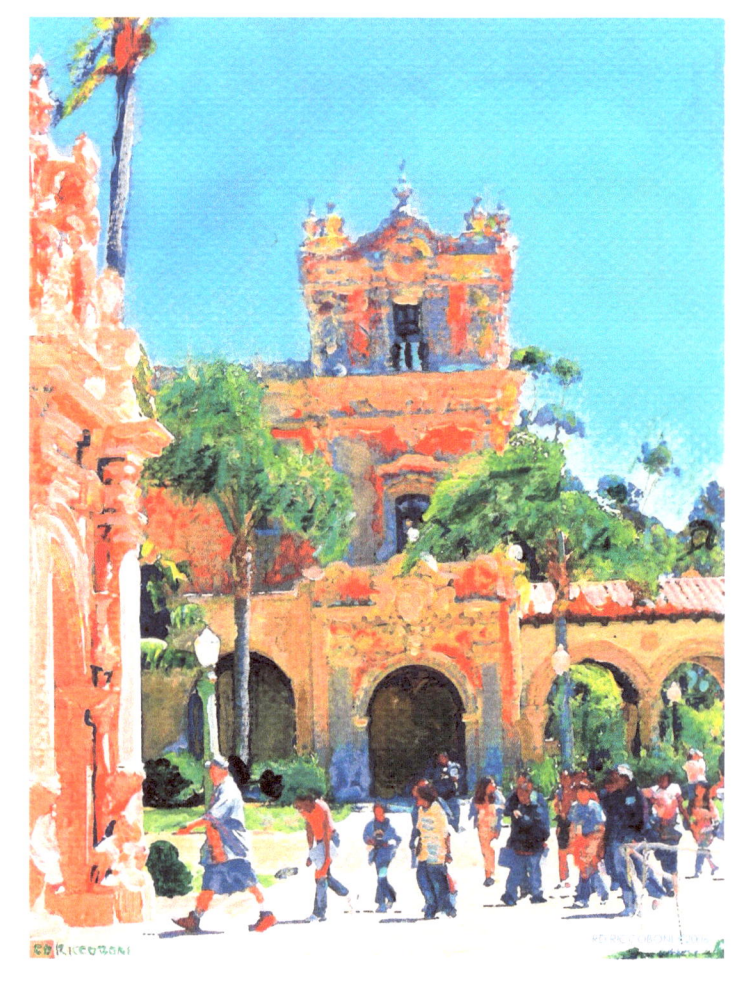

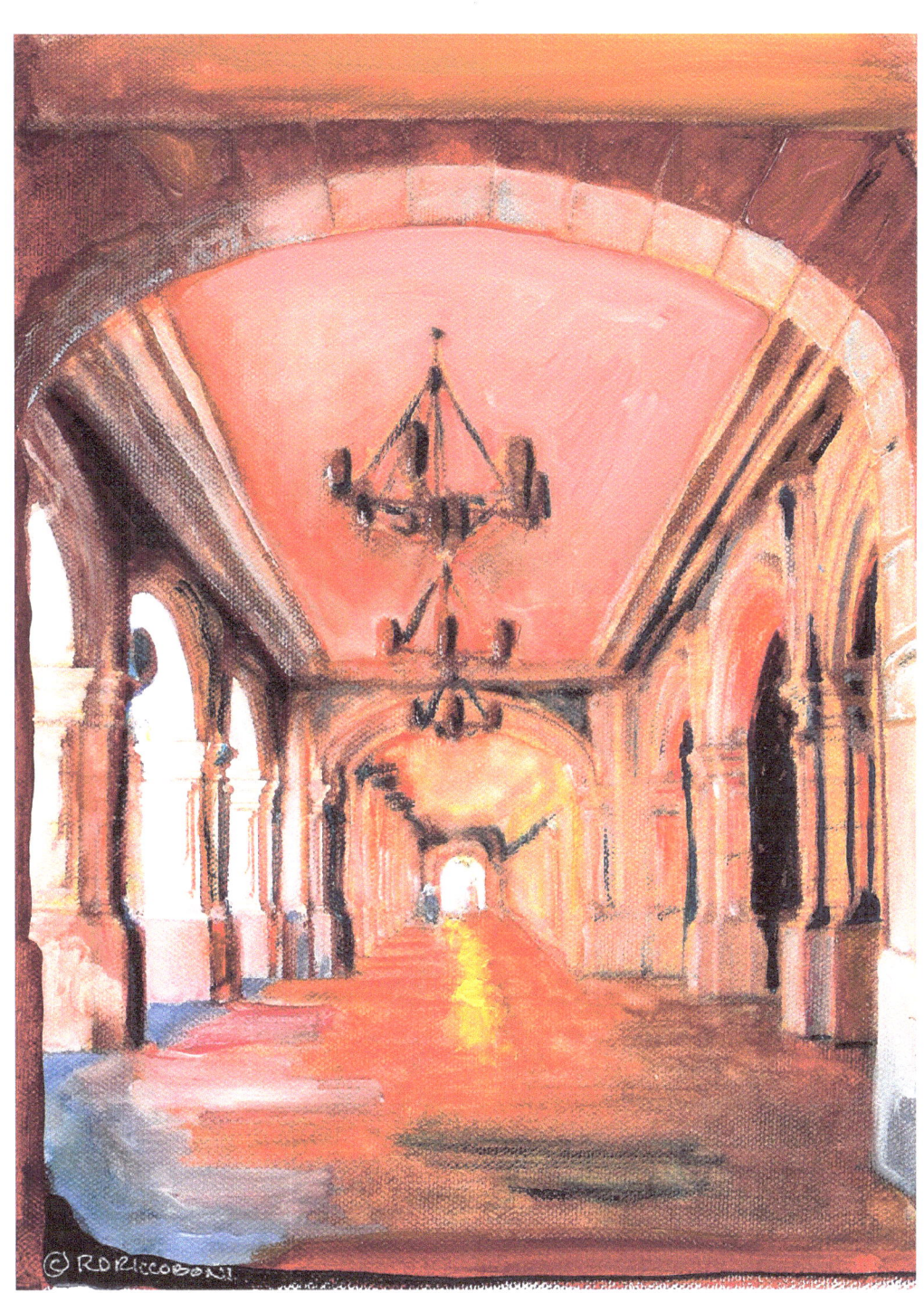

© RDRiccoboni

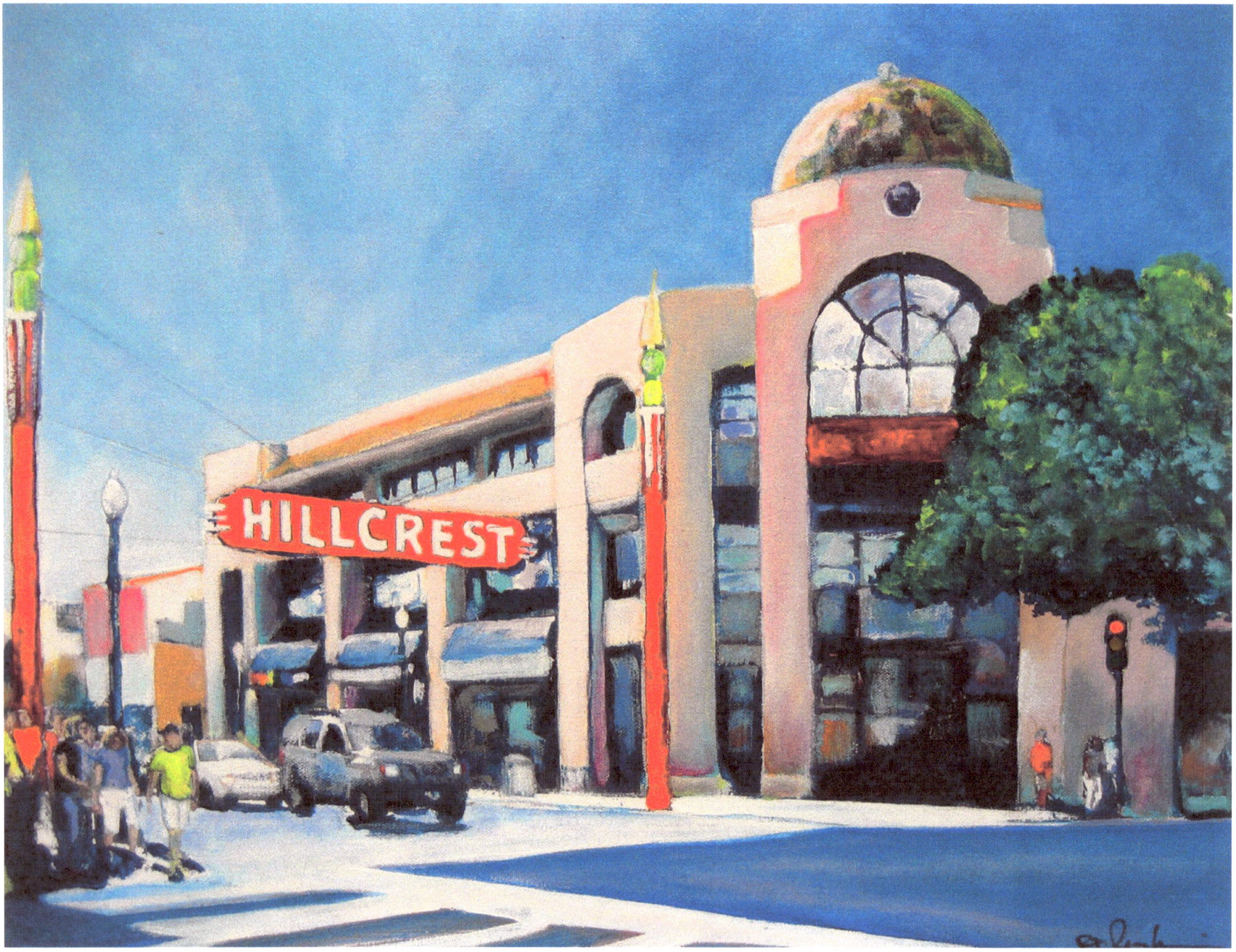

Above: **Hillcrest**

Right: **North Park**

Following page right.

Left: **La Jolla Palms - Scripps Park**

Right: **Panarama Drive,** University Heights

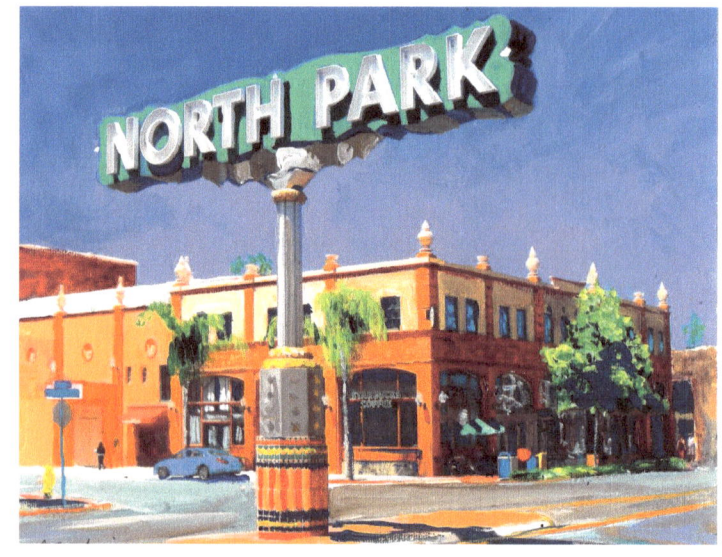

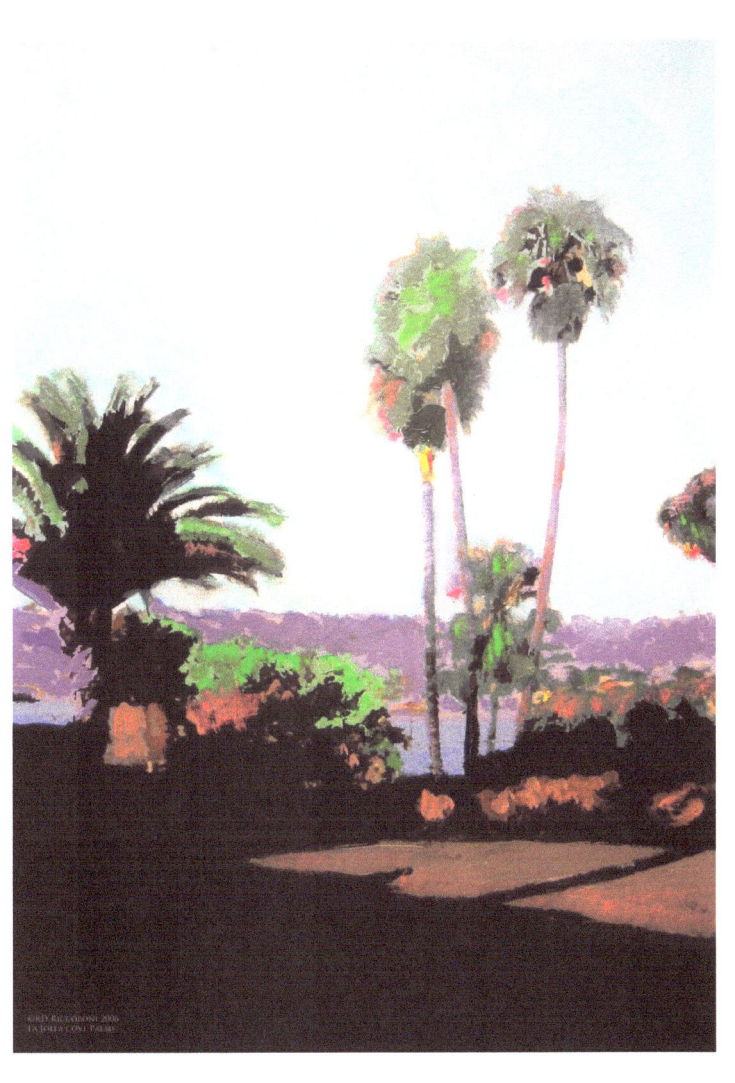 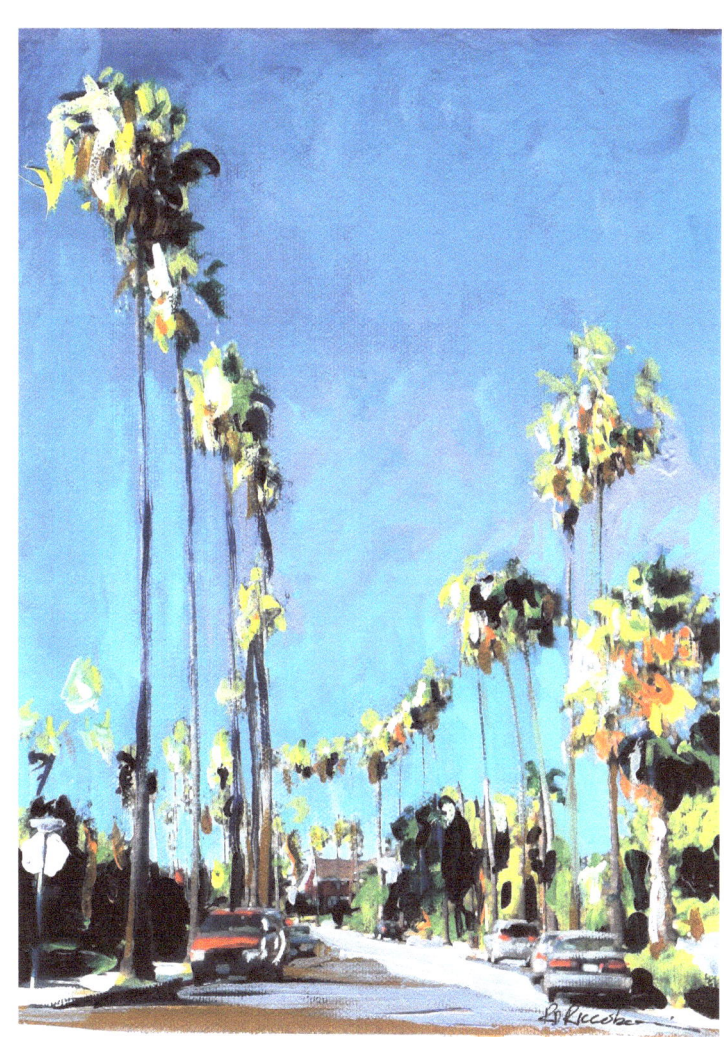

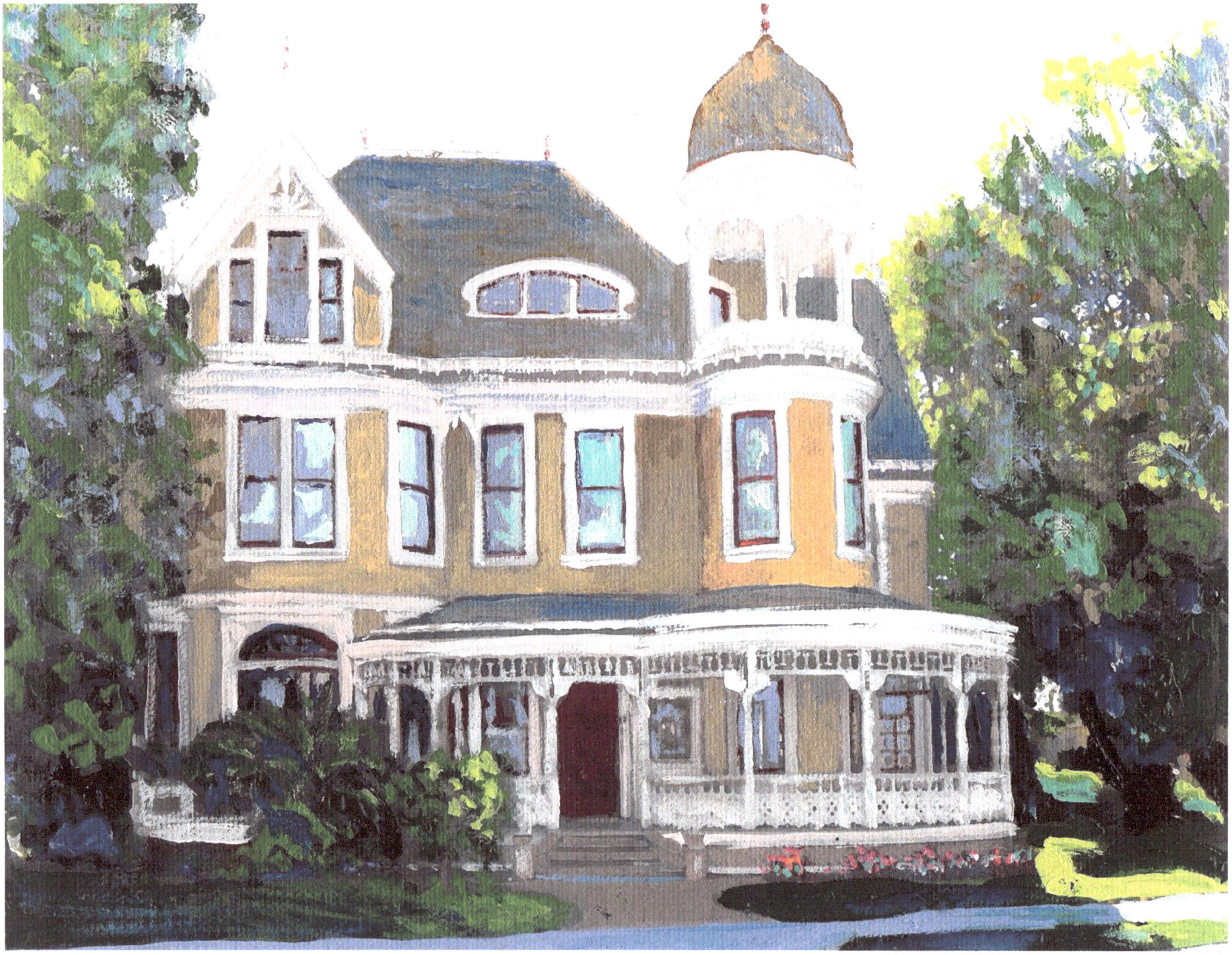

Bankers Hill
Above: **The Waterman House**
Below Right: **The Timken House**

Following page right:

Left: **Sidewalk Cafe on Coronado Island**

Right, **Towers in Little Italy, San Diego**

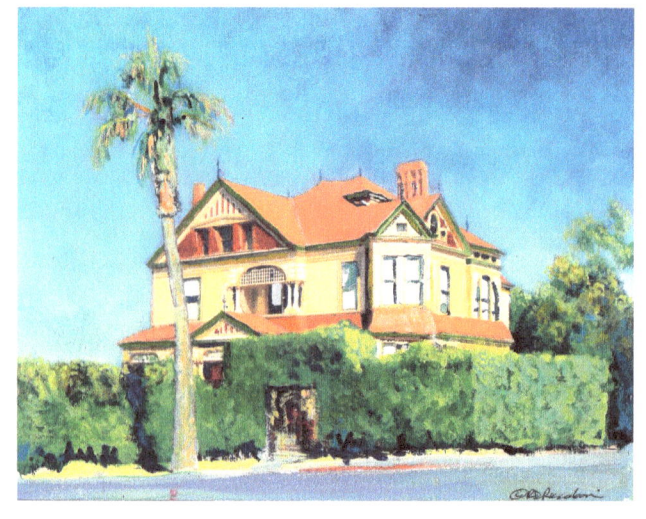

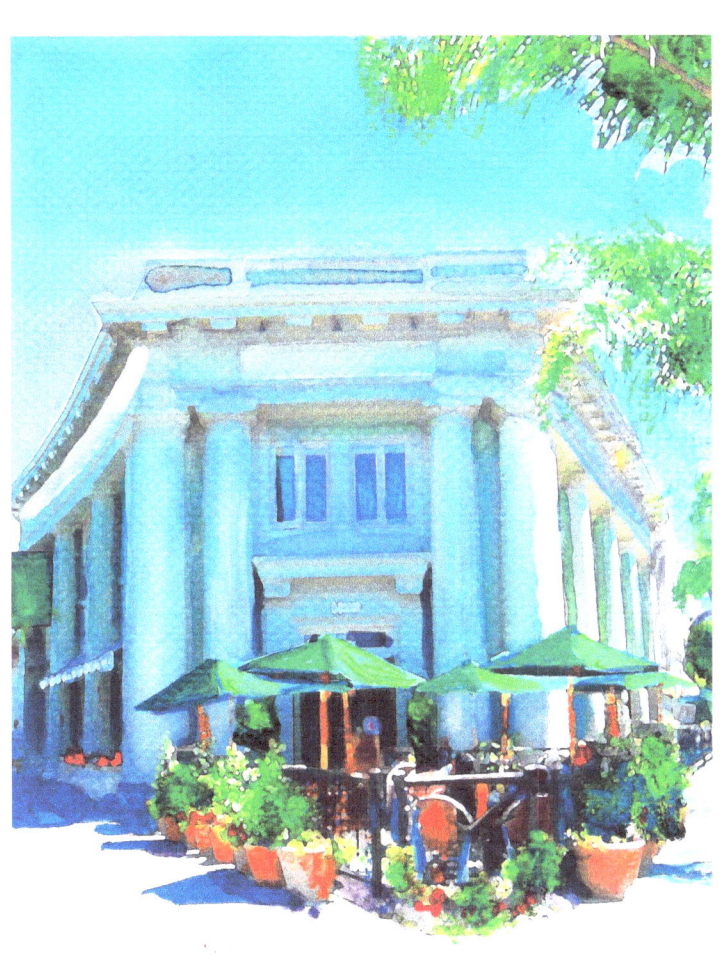

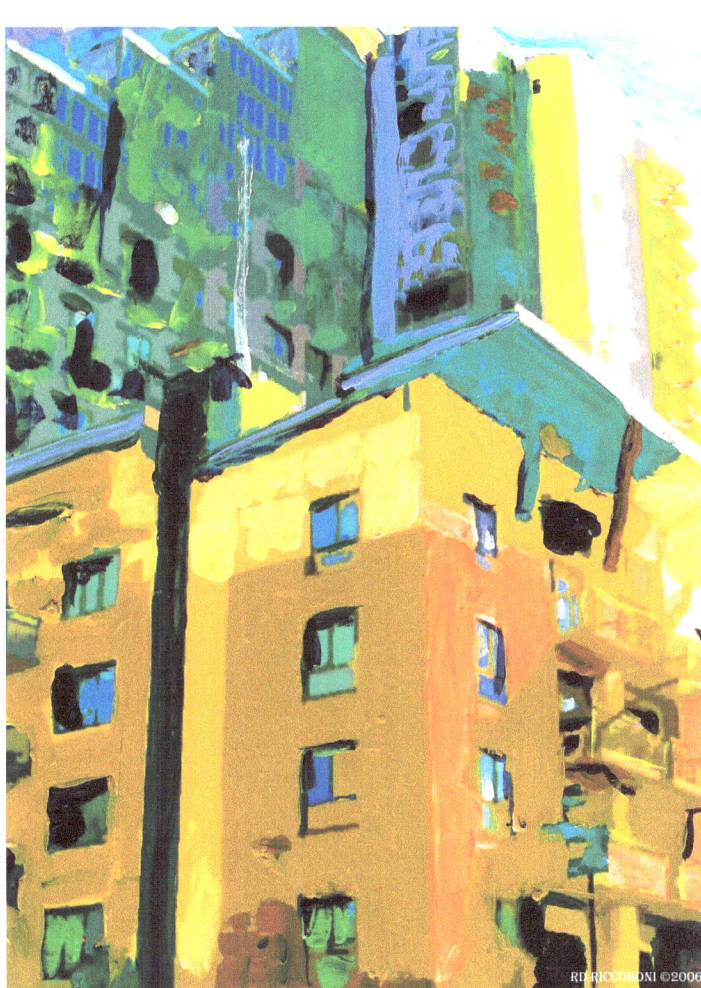

RD RICCOBONI ©2006

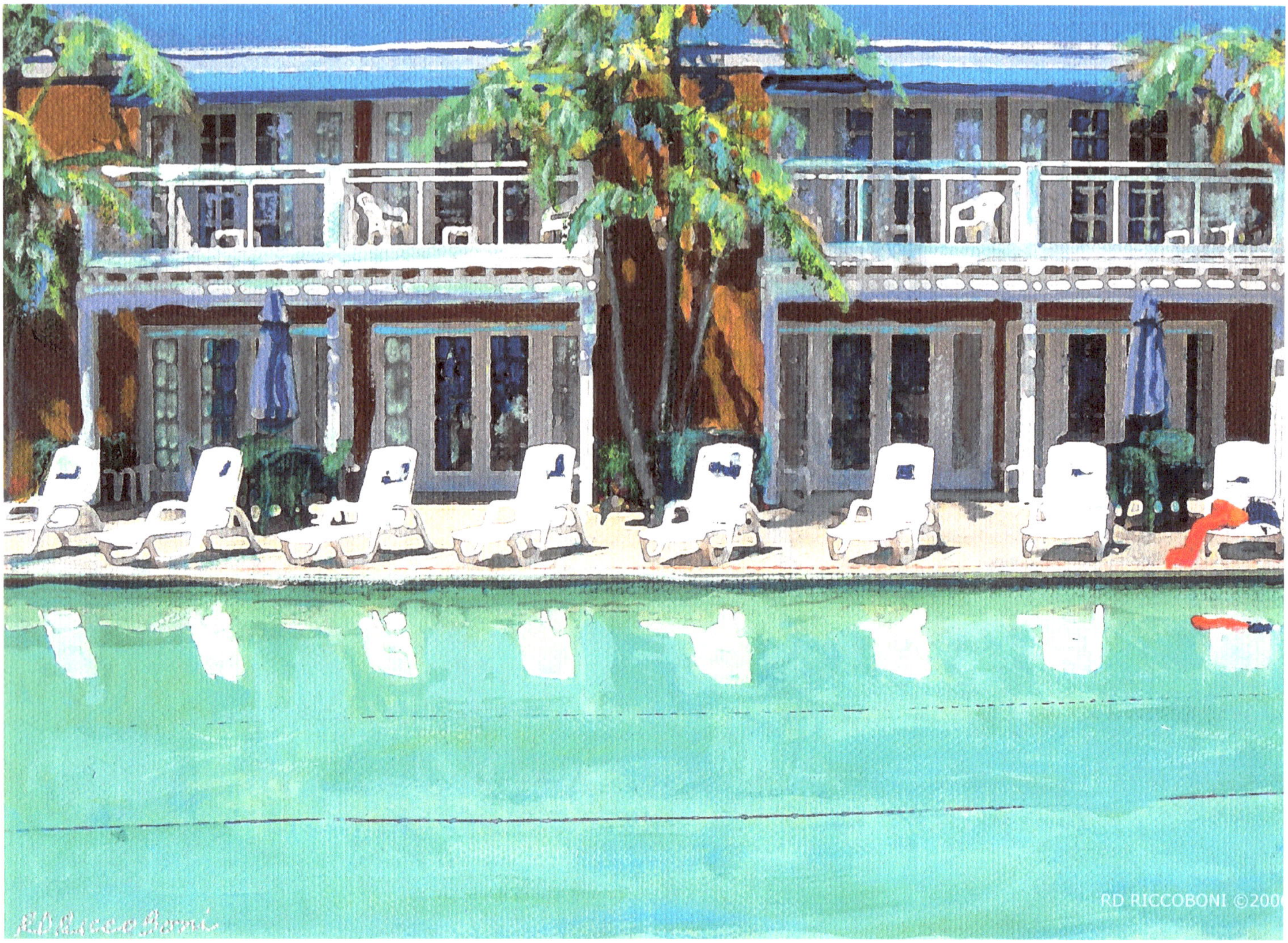

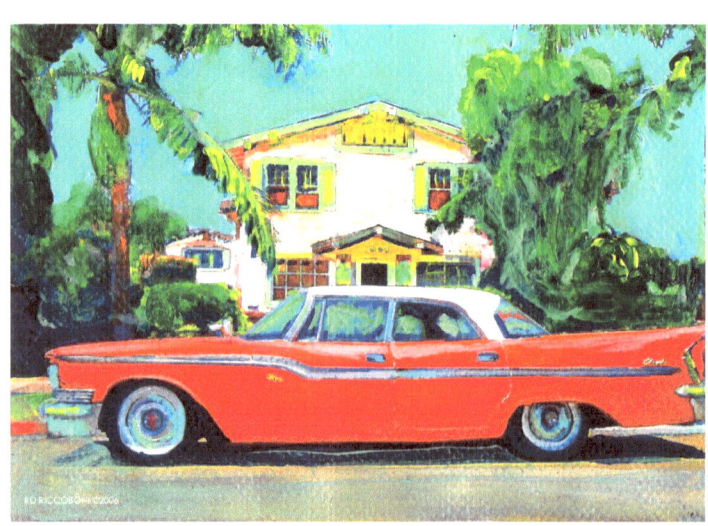

Above: **Poolside at The Lafayette Hotel**

Left: **The Red Sled**

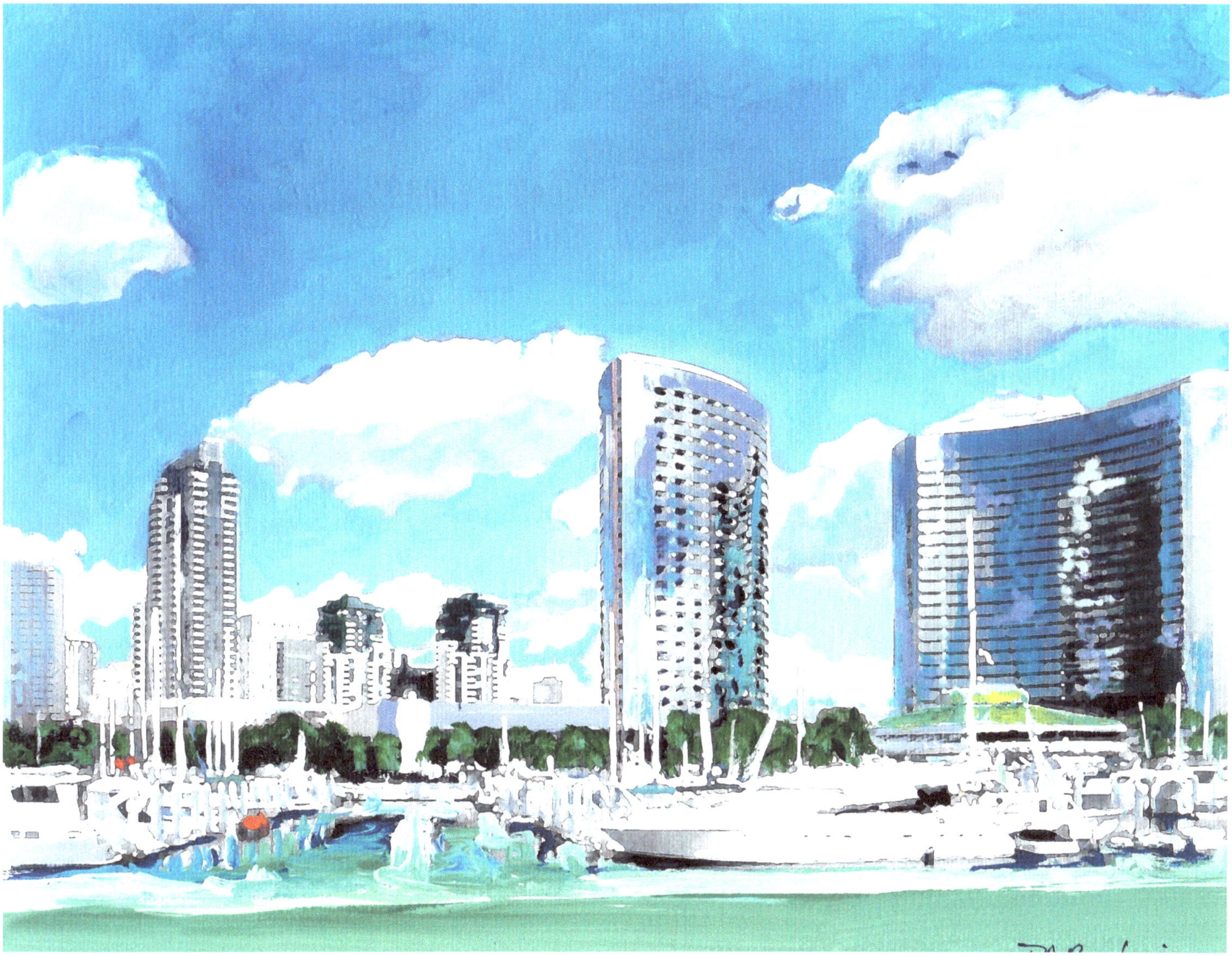

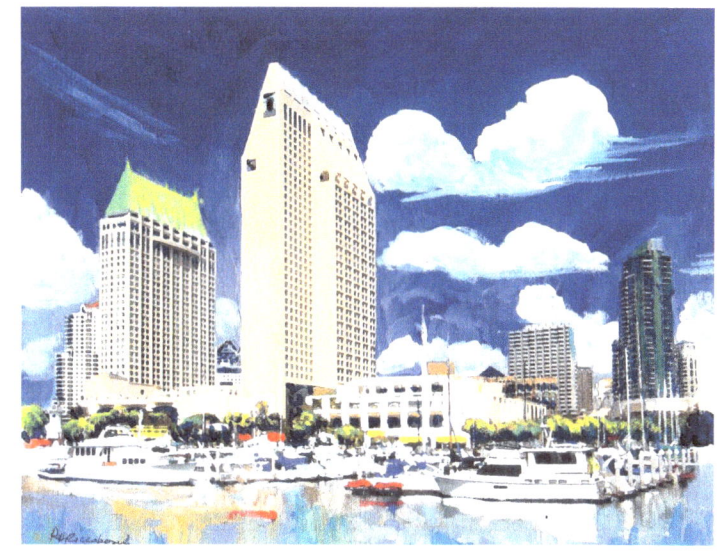

New Town

Above: *San Diego Marina*

Lower right: *Boats in the San Diego Marina along the Embarcadero.*

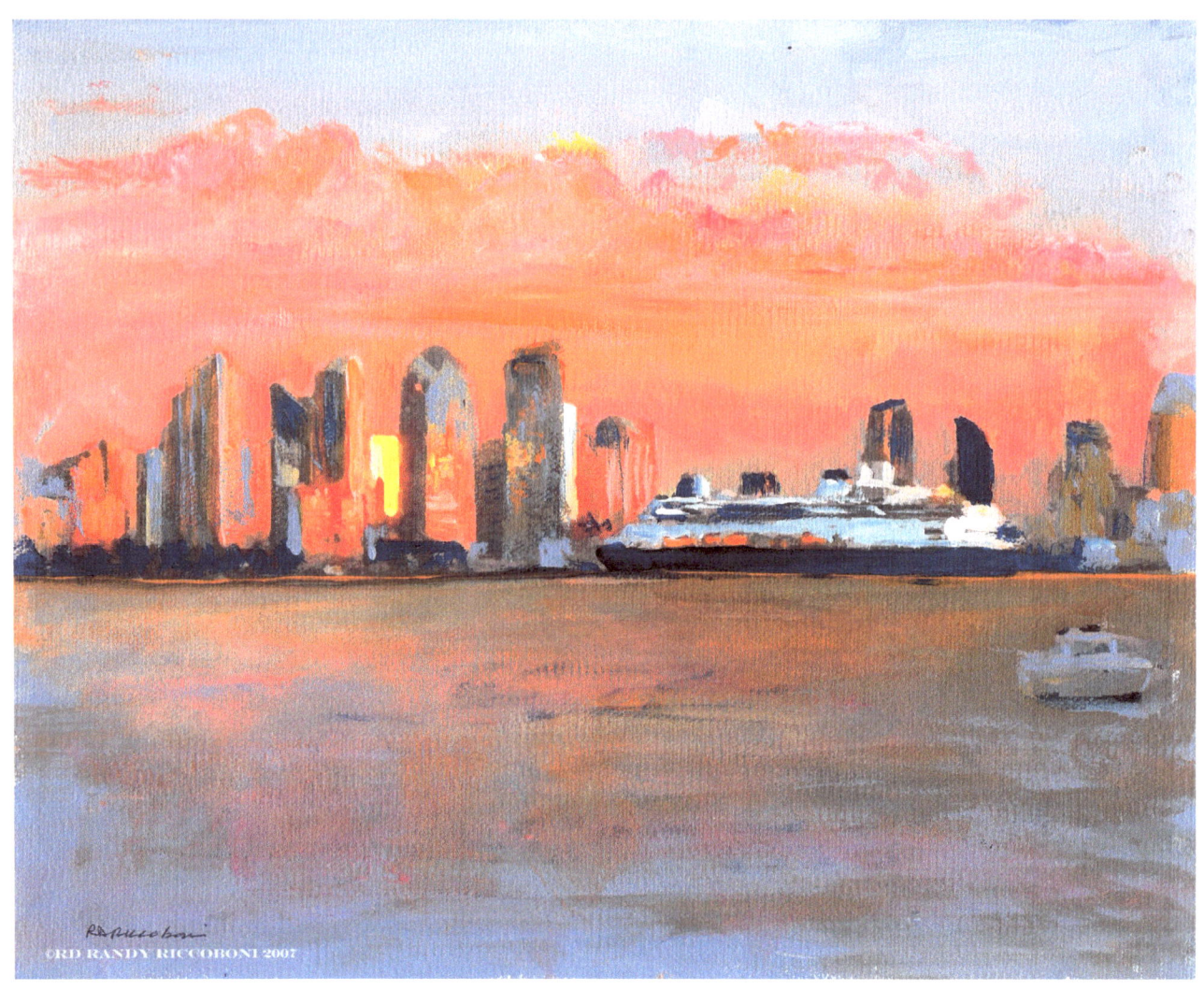

Sunset from Harbor Island

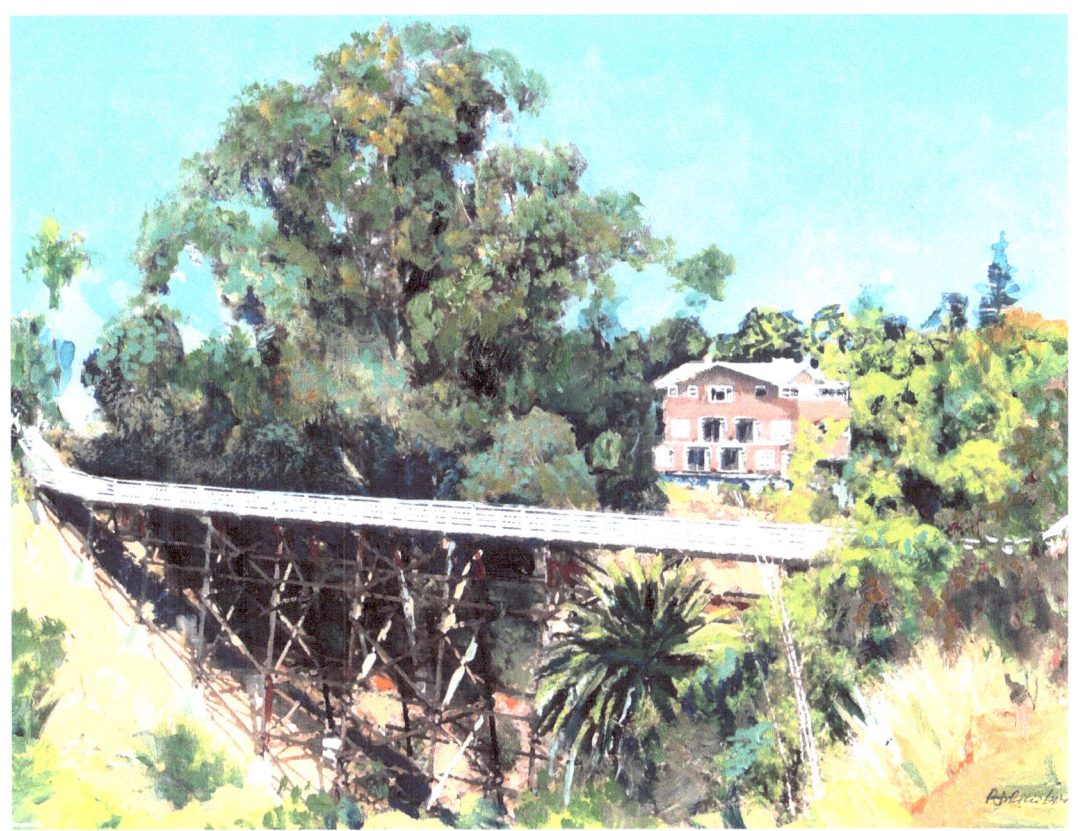

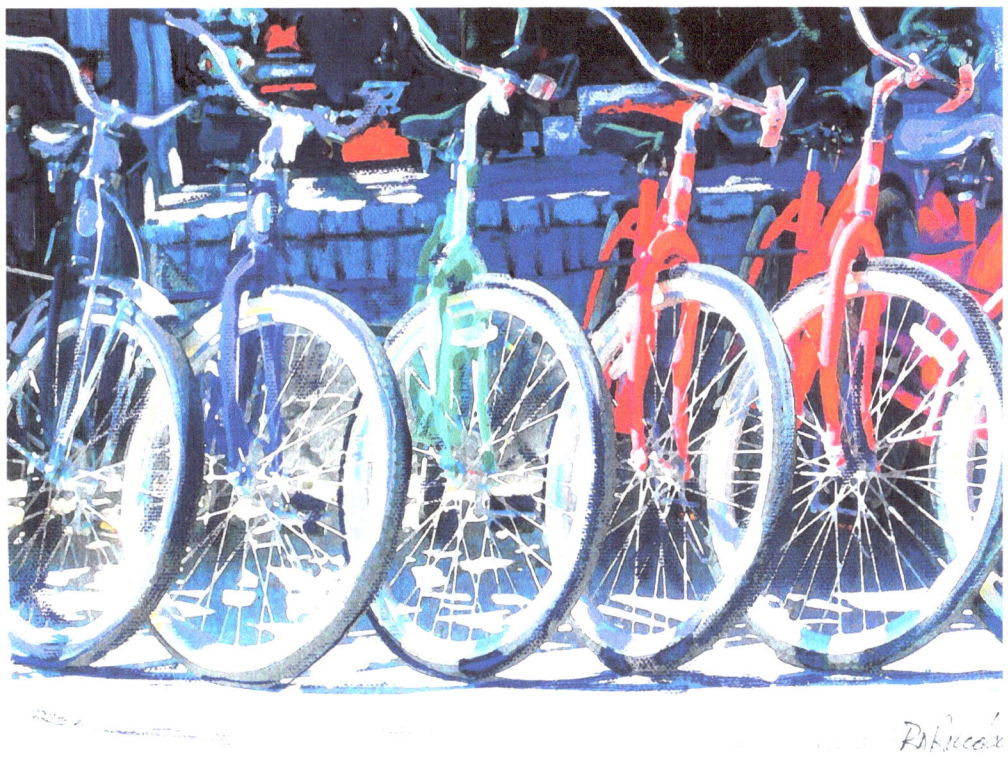

Above: **Maple canyon and the Quince Street Bridge,**
Bankers Hill

Below: **Bicycles in a Row**, University Heights

Discover the beautiful art of California painter RD Riccoboni®.
Known to many as the painter of love, joy and happiness.

One of California's favorite artists Riccoboni is an innovative American painter (born in
Fresno, California, 1960), influenced by his early years living in the suburbs of New York
City. A self-taught artist, he credits encouragement by family and teachers for his drive and
inspiration. Riccoboni is an internationally collected artist and best-selling author. The results
of his career have been astounding and in 2007 Riccoboni founded the popular Beacon
Artworks Gallery at the beautiful Fiesta de Reyes in San Diego's Old Town State Historic Park.

The colorful paintings of RD Riccoboni® on canvas and paper depict his travels and local
interest. Subjects include California landscape, cityscape, portraiture, street-scenes, public
events, local happenings and friends. His vivid palette is derived from the bold colors of the
original rainbow flag. These colors represent, sexuality, health, sunshine, nature, art,
harmony and spirit. Riccoboni's internationally recognized work represents community, a
sense of place in a positive and life affirming manner.

A fan of architecture, Mr. Riccoboni is currently working on drawings and paintings of
historic American buildings and landscape that is vanishing.

"I am constantly asked what drives and inspires me. My answer is usually, forward thinking
and working from the heart with love and feeling the positive and beautiful vibrations of
color, contrast, new perspectives and spirit that surround our daily lives."

See more of Riccoboni's art works, paintings, drawings at:
Beacon Artworks Gallery in San Diego California

and online at:

Beacon-artworks.com

Everydayintentions.com

www.ingramcontent.com/pod-product-compliance
Lightning Source LLC
Chambersburg PA
CBHW051056180526
45172CB00002B/660